Understanding
The Great Tribulation
and the Era of Peace

Understanding
The Great Tribulation
and the Era of Peace

**Some of the Messages Given
to John Leary by Our Divine Lord**

1993 – 2000

As recorded in his books

*Prepare for the Great Tribulation
and the Era of Peace*

Volumes I to XV,
and as taken from the Internet from July 1999

John Rochford

Queenship

PUBLISHING COMPANY
P.O. Box 220 • Goleta, CA 93116
(800) 647-9882 • (805) 692-0043 • Fax: (805) 967-5843

"It is only when you see with the eyes of faith and hear with love in your heart, that one understands the message I am sending. Do not have doubts, My son, when I have shown you the way."

— Message of 13 August 1995

Library of Congress Number # 00-134983

Published by:
    Queenship Publishing
    P.O. Box 220
    Goleta, CA 93116
    (800) 647-9882 • (805) 692-0043 • Fax: (805) 967-5843
    http://www.queenship.org

Printed in the United States of America

ISBN: 1-57918-142-2

Declaration

The decree of the Congregation for the Propagation of the Faith, A.A.S.58, 1186 (approved by Pope Paul VI on 14 October 1966), states that the Nihil Obstat and Imprimatur are no longer required on publications that deal with new apparitions, revelations, prophesies or miracles, provided they contain nothing contrary to faith and morals.

The publisher recognises and accepts that the final authority regarding the messages in this book rests with the Holy See, to whose judgement we willingly submit.

Statement by His Holiness, Pope Urban VIII:

"In cases which concern private revelation, it is better to believe than not believe, for if you believe, and it is proven true, you will be happy that you have believed, because our Holy Mother asked it. If you believe, and it should be proven false, you will receive all blessings as if it had been true, because you believed it to be true."

(Pope Urban VIII, 1623-44)

Chapter II, No. 12 of the Second Vatican Council's *"Lumen Gentium"* states that "...the holy spirit makes the people holy, leads them and enriches them with his virtues. Allotting his gifts 'at will to each individual' (1 Cor 12:11) he also distributes special graces among the faithful of every rank ... Those who have charge over the church should judge the genuineness and orderly use of these gifts, and it is especially their office not indeed to extinguish the spirit, but to test all things and hold fast to what is good. (see 1 Th 5:12 and 19-21)

Contents

Introduction ix

Part I: "The Warning" to "The Era of Peace" 1
    Index to Part I 3
    The Messages 11

Part II: Supplementary Messages 98
    Index to Part II 91
    The Messages 96

Part III: Alphabetical Reference to Some Messages   139

Part IV: Preparation to go into Hiding 225

Message to Australia: Thursday 17 June 1997

Mary said: *"My dear children, thank you for your many rosaries tonight. I will raise up your prayers to my Son for your petitions. Because of your prayers, I will raise up Australia before my Son as well. People of Australia, listen to my requests. By the power of your rosaries, you will hold up my mantle of protection against the evils of your land. If there is not enough prayer, you will lessen my protection. So pray my three rosaries each day and say my consecration prayers, so all of your souls may be close to my Son's Heart. Seek His love, my children, and all else will be given to you."*

Introduction

John Leary is a retired chemist who lives with his wife, Carol, in the suburbs of Rochester, New York, in the USA. John has been a daily communicant since the age of seventeen. He recites the fifteen decades of the Rosary daily.

In April 1993, John and Carol made a pilgrimage to Our Lady's shrine at Medjugorje in Yugoslavia. It was while he was at Medjugorje that John received the first indication from Our Divine Lord that he wished to call him to undertake a special work for Him. Since July 1993, John has been receiving interior visions and messages from God the Father, the Holy Spirit, the Blessed Virgin Mary, his guardian angel and many of the saints.

Our Divine Lord's messages to John Leary — as recorded in his books *Prepare for the Great Tribulation and the Era of Peace* — and to all who are privileged to read and accept them as the words of Jesus, are messages of love, hope and forgiveness of an infinitely caring and compassionate God. They represent a whole way of life for each one of us: a "road map" to eternal happiness. That Our Divine Lord should come to reveal to us the events facing us in the very near future, and that He should also come to show us how we might prepare for those events and thus save our souls, is indeed a gift we can never be thankful enough for.

However, a simple reading of the attached collection of messages does not in any way do justice to the Divine author's intentions. It must be remembered that Our Divine Lord, in His infinite wisdom, chose to give a whole series of messages to John Leary, spread over a number of years. We cannot possibly come to an understanding of the fullness of the Lord's messages if we confine our readings to those in this book, the purpose of which is to give the reader directed access to some of the messages from Our Divine Lord which, at this time, would seem to take on an added sense of urgency.

The purpose of this book is also to help bring about an understanding of the "Great Tribulation" and the "Era of Peace," by presenting some of the messages given to John Leary in a single volume. Hopefully, this will facilitate and encourage a wide reading of those messages.

In presenting these messages, I have felt it necessary to be absolutely faithful to Our Divine Lord and to preserve His messages to the extent possible so that they may be understood as Our Divine Lord intended. It has not been possible, of course, to include all of each message on all of the subjects included herein. Nor has it been possible to include some messages on all issues which John Leary has recorded in his books.

For this reason, it is most strongly recommended that all who read these messages also obtain a copy of John Leary's books, and thereby profit by the greater spiritual understanding that will flow from such reading. To facilitate further reading, the Volume and Page number references to John Leary's books are shown along with each message herein.

All emphasis in bold or italic type within quotations, or other forms of highlighting of particular messages, is mine, not John Leary's, as is the insertion of references to Scripture or quotations from Scripture at the beginning of some chapters.

I would like to point out that, in giving these messages to John Leary, Our Divine Lord does not present them to the exclusion of the Church or Scripture. Indeed, He calls on us many times in His messages to be faithful to the Church and to read Scripture. In this respect, the following message to John Leary of *5 October 1994* is worth noting:

"If you long to know the coming events, read Revelation, Exodus and the other prophetic books. Listen to the Church's interpretation of the Bible and discern the meaning of My word. Everything you need for salvation has been revealed to you there."

John Rochford

Note: *Fifteen volumes of the messages have been printed as of March 2000. These cover the years 1993/94 to 30 June 1999. Apart from volumes I to III (which each cover one year's messages), the volumes cover three months at a time and are very easy to read.*

Part I

"The Warning" to "The Era of Peace"

The Warning 1

The Famine 2

Pope John Paul II 10

The Mark of the Beast — The Chip 18

The Antichrist 22

The Need to go into Hiding 35

The Plagues — of Locusts, Scorpions and Snakes . . 42

Electronic Communications — TV, Radio,
       Computers, the Internet, Motor Vehicles 44

The Tribulation — Comets, Earthquakes, Volcanoes . 49

Armageddon 58

The Era of Peace 64

Understanding the Great Tribulation and the Era of Peace

Index to Some of the Messages to John Leary — Part I

The Warning

Page **Subject**

11 No misunderstanding. All will know God. Antichrist follows the warning.

12 Time will be suspended. Understanding of good and bad actions. Knowledge of sin, truth and our offences against God.

13 Hell — a frightening experience. Don't listen to the devil. Prepare to join Jesus before the warning — a period of grace after the warning.

14 Many will not change after the warning but will know their defiance of God. A time for conversion and reparation. The Sacrament of Reconciliation — our only hope.

15 After the warning — no middle ground. The choice is for God or against God. Nothing is secret from God — all our deeds exposed. A new consciousness — we will see all our life's experiences.

17 Many will be left in a state of shock. Refusal to change — condemnation to hell.

The Famine

Page **Subject**

17 Have faith and trust in Jesus to provide. Put aside food and water. The miracle of food replication.

18 Food shortages a contrived means to control people. Multiplication of food for survival. A massive world depression — third world countries first.

20 Reliance on food set aside — Roving bands seeking food. Increasing difficulty to buy and sell. Increasing weather problems. Save one year's supply of food and water.

Pope John Paul II and the Imposter Pope

Page   **Subject**

21   Major upheaval and schism in the Church. Exile of the Pope. Some shepherds are like sheep in wolves' clothing.

22   Exile of the Pope (on the thirteenth of some month) during political upheaval in Italy.

22   Listen to Pope John Paul II — He is the Pope for these times. Election of evil pope. He will mislead the people.

23   The imposter pope will follow the Antichrist. Do not believe him. Beware of the imposter pope. He will be full of deception.

24   Remain faithful to the Church established by the apostles. Mary will watch over Pope John Paul II as he leads the remnant Church. The imposter pope will violate Church traditions and Dogmas.

26   Revolt of bishops and cardinals. Do not be deceived. Follow only Pope John Paul II as successor to the apostles.

27   Preserve the teachings of the Church, as given by the apostles. Pray for Pope John Paul II — the last faithful Pope before the Antichrist.

28   All will have to choose either John Paul II or the imposter. Underground masses will be necessary. Pray for discernment.

29   The imposter — the false witness of the Book of Revelation. Go into hiding when the Pope leaves Rome.

The Mark of the Beast — the Chip

Page   **Subject**

30   Refuse the mark, even under pain of death — trust in Jesus. The hypnotic state of those with the chip.

31   Smart cards with the chip — reject these even if you cannot buy or sell. Antichrist unable to find those who don't take the chip. Need to go into hiding to avoid detention centres.

32   Antichrist declaration when satellites and chips in place. Three signs of when to go into hiding. Don't be deceived by advertising for the chip in the hand.

33   Low orbit communication satellites — monitoring of every move. Restriction on travel, jobs, buying and selling. Satan's deception — don't be misled by claims of peace. Be prepared to die rather than take the chip. Jesus will provide if we trust in Him.

The Antichrist

Page   **Subject**

35   Control of minds — Demonic powers. Conjunction of stars — a sign of the Antichrist's coming to power.

35   The mark on the forehead — recognition of God's people. Underground Masses — Rosaries our only weapon. Events will speed up. Protection for houses of constant prayer. Evil bishops and cardinals — Exile of Pope John Paul II.

36   A time of chaos — Entrance of the Antichrist as a man of peace. Need to pray for discernment. Form prayer groups. Seek out underground Masses to avoid heretical teachings.

38   Antichrist — appearance of a peacemaker. A tyrannical ruler, intent on destruction. The need to flee the cities. Torture and martyrdom.

39   Prayer groups. Jesus' cross our protection — wear it. Arrival of Antichrist after the warning. Pray constantly. Antichrist — use of technology, TV, virtual reality. Help of St. Michael.

40   The two beasts — the false pope and the Antichrist. Do not take up arms in these evil days. False prophets — discern very carefully. Signs and wonders will announce the Antichrist — An eclipse.

41   Pink lightning — power of the Antichrist. Persecution — build up spiritual strength now. Be prepared for Jesus' Second Coming. Pray and fast now.

42   Unheard of display of power. Seek help of our guardian angels. Those who knowingly take the mark of the beast. Antichrist — miraculous powers. The devil incarnate. Antichrist's agents — identification of Christians for elimination.

43   Seek Jesus' mercy and help to survive. Antichrist — search by satellites and helicopters. Jesus' miracles to protect the faithful. Another sign of the Antichrist: blue light in the sky.

44   Crowd control via helicopter. Not told these things to frighten. Those who refuse to prepare will be found wanting. Unusual light sources — illusion of miraculous powers.

45   Antichrist's declaration — power in literature and pictures. Lasers — for special effects. Churches destroyed in the persecution. Even some of the elect will be mislead. Establish prayer groups. Those refusing Jesus' help may be lost. **Antichrist's declaration** . Cables, TV, faxes, computers, copiers etc.

47   When to go into hiding — **no credit cards, smart cards or those with the chip.** The tribulation. Antichrist's declaration — Announcement imminent. G7 meeting — plot for takeover in readiness for Antichrist.

48   Confession, sacramentals and physical needs to leave. The year of 666 — the sign of the Antichrist (666 x 3 = 1998). New money system and world government. Continuing disasters.

The Need to go Into Hiding

Page   **Subject**

49   Jesus will instruct us where to go. Pray to Jesus for help and to find a safe haven. Be faithful. Do not worry about what to eat or where to stay. Jesus will provide.

50   Do not fear. Take some basic necessities. Remain faithful to Jesus and He will lead us. Be ready to go after the warning. Take a shovel. We must put our trust in Jesus — don't worry about where to go.

51   Take into hiding spiritual weapons and a few earthly helps. Do not worry about what to bring. Jesus will provide. Pray for help. Pray to our guardian angels to direct us. Electronic search instruments will be confused. Tracker dogs will not find us. Pray for discernment and help.

52   Reasons to be in hiding. A testing time. Pray and trust in Jesus. All movements will be watched. Pray for protection. The permanent signs in the sky to mark safe havens. Pray much to be faithful. Powers of Antichrist. Strange lights from heaven. Powers of suggestion.

54   Difficulty of travel — scanning for the mark of the beast. Be in hiding. Great faith needed to save our souls. A time of purification.

55   Jesus' help — an urge to hide for our own safety. Pray much for conversion of souls. Hibernation during the tribulation. Be prepared to leave everything and follow our angels.

56   Scorn of these messages. Follow Jesus. Three signs of when to go into hiding. They who hesitate to go may risk capture in detention centres. Leave your possessions. Take into hiding only what you can carry.

Plagues of Locusts, Scorpions and Snakes

Page   **Subject**
57   Pestilence and plagues of locusts and scorpions.
58   Plagues of Snakes

Electronic Communications — TV, Radio, Computers, Internet, and Motor Vehicles

Page   **Subject**
59   TV sets must be off when Antichrist comes. He will control minds through TV. Hypnotism, demonic powers, electrical devices. Manipulation of TV images. Virtual reality over TV.

60   Avoid use of Internet. Immorality of TV comedy. Increasing thresholds of wickedness. Concern about use of Internet — a tool of the evil one. Subliminal messages. Avoid its use.

61   Don't use Internet for personal messages. Dispense with all electronic communications at the time of the tribulation. Car number plates — special tracking devices. Low orbit satellites — ability to track and immobilise new cars.

62   Detection devices in cars. Monitoring of public access lines. Loss of privacy and security. Computers and TV — built-in means for two-way communication, even when turned off.

63   Transponders in newer cars for tracking. What to do after the Antichrist's declaration. Three signs of when to go into hiding.

The Tribulation — Comets, Earthquakes, Volcanoes, Diseases, Weather Control

Page	Subject
64	**The Atlantic Comet** — three days darkness. Events to speed up dramatically. Threat of WWIII. Spiritual chaos reflected in the weather. Shortening of Antichrist's reign. Demons loosed from Hell.
66	Comet of Jesus' judgement now on track for earth. Evil in the world. The chastisement — closeness of the Comet. Resulting fumes. Difficulty to breathe.
67	**Change in the Earth's orbit**. A great coldness: prepare with warm clothes. Volcanic eruptions. Distortion of the earth's crust. Change in the magnetic poles. Increasing frequency and intensity of earthquakes. Work to save souls.
68	Contagious diseases. **Blood red moon:** a sign of the tribulation. Tesla weather machines. Weather and food manipulation. **Speed up of events**: few will understand. Let Jesus rule our lives.
69	Jesus' Second Coming. Return to confession. The comet — in the Atlantic. Beginning of three days darkness. The comet — announcement by astronomers. Many lives lost.
70	The comet — already on its way. Angels will deflect attempts to destroy it. **Volcanoes, huge earthquakes — will reshape the dry land**. Much death and destruction. The violence in the weather reflects violence in society. California earthquake.
71	Quick succession of events. Trust in Jesus' protection. Diseases and pestilence. Vaccine resistant strains of germs. Much terror and chaos. The comet - much dust and ash. The sun blotted out. Only blessed candles will do. The Era of Peace follows the comet.
73	Drug resistant mutations of diseases. Mutations added to older diseases. Epidemics of air-borne diseases. Lack of medicines. Cure at caves and safe havens.
73	Germ warfare. Healing of plagues and diseases. Protection at safe havens and caves.

Armageddon

Page	Subject
74	Unrest in the Middle East will culminate in the battle of Armageddon. All the people of the earth will be drawn into the conflict.
76	Many angels will be in the battle led by St. Michael. Gas and oil shortages. Many things will be horse driven.
76	Angels able to defend the faithful with full force of their power. Israel — the land of the Battle of Armageddon. Satan's time about to end. The Antichrist's declaration is not far off.
77	The site of the Battle of Armageddon. The demons and the evil men will be chained in hell. Iraq — its use by the one-world people. Muslims and communist nations to unite against the West.
78	The evil men and the demons against the faithful warriors. Satan will be defeated and he and his forces will be chained in hell. Trust in Jesus' help.
79	The power of the angels. Listen to their prompting. The Battle of Armageddon and the Era of Peace.

The Era of Peace

Page	Subject
80	The promise of My Kingdom is upon you. You will clearly see Me and your joy will know no bounds. **It will come in John Leary's lifetime** — but at a high price of endurance.
81	It will come with Mary's triumph. Many will be tested to the limit. After Mary's triumph it will be as for the Garden of Eden. A dramatic facelift of the earth. Restoration to its former beauty. No evil, no anger, no sickness, no death, no killing.
83	Abundance of food. No need to work to eat. A taste of heaven before the final judgement.
84	Full knowledge and understanding of the renewed earth. All will be in harmony. Animals will not kill each other. Man will not need to eat. A beauty among nature beyond our wildest dreams. Every animal will be precious.

85   The old will look younger. Children will mature in their thirties. All in perfect harmony. No wars. Only the faithful brought back to life will have glorified bodies. Glorified bodies of those who died. Those faithful through the tribulation will have rejuvenated bodies.

86   The New Jerusalem. The temperature will be perfect. Full knowledge and understanding of life. Temples of light and places of worship — anytime day or night. No fear of animals. The age we live in will become the New Era of Peace. The New Jerusalem.

Some of the Messages Given to John Leary by Our Divine Lord — 1993 to 1999

as recorded in his books

Prepare for the Great Tribulation and the Era of Peace

1. The Warning

Volume II — Jul '94 to Jun '95

No misunderstanding. All will know God. Antichrist follows the warning

P30 — "This will be a revelation to many who did not believe in God and to those who knew God but have become lukewarm. It will be a time where everyone will understand that they will have one last chance to choose Me or the devil in the world. There will be no misunderstanding or any excuse for everyone not to know. Some will have the fear of God awaken their soul and return to confession, while others will reject it as a dream. All will see themselves in the light of their own sins and have to answer to Me and their consciences. After this event you will see the entrance of the Antichrist as he will come to power."

P78 — "Woe unto you, O people of the earth. I have said: 'When I return, shall I find any faith on the earth?' Your generation has been very much attacked by the devil. His deeds are everywhere to be seen in your many abominations. For this reason of your plight, I will offer you one last chance to choose Me on terms where you cannot refute My presence. Nor will you not know of My existence. With this warning you will come face to face with your Lord to show you all your sins and how they offend Me. At that moment you all will have an opportunity to either choose Me or the world. Take time, though, to judge your actions for your decision now will be final with no grey areas and no excuses will be taken after this. For you will truly see Me as I am in My glory. There will be no doubt about which you are choosing. 'Choose life', therefore, that you may be with Me forever in My graces and splendour. Otherwise, a choice of the world will leave you empty with eternal chaos in hell and no hope of ever finding My peace. This will be the most important choice you will ever make in your lifetime, so choose wisely."

Volume III — Jul '95 to Jun '96:

Time will be suspended. Understanding of good and bad actions

P9 — "My son, you are witnessing My warning, as I have shown you many times before. This time, I will explain a little more of what you will experience. You will see time suspended, and all at once you will come before Me. In that moment, there will be no doubt that this is a supernatural event. It will seem to you almost like a judgement time, where you will have a full cognizance of My love and My mercy. Then will appear before you, almost like a book, where your life up to then will have been written, and the remaining chapters unwritten, of the rest of your life. Then slowly, with no sense of time, you will see each moment of your life portrayed to you as I would see it. You will understand all your good and bad actions and see the motives and intentions of those actions.

"You will be able to appreciate in a short time, how much of your life that you have given up to Me. Some will be taken aback to understand how little time you gave to Me in each day. From that day forward, you will see a choice, which I will offer to each of you. You can continue on as you have, or you can understand how you can please Me even more than you have. By showing Me your love in your daily actions, you will be given one last opportunity to redirect your lives. This is why those in great sin, will have a rude awakening of how evil they have been."

Knowledge of sin, truth and our offences against God.

"Now you will see one beautiful chance to redirect your lives, before it is too late and you lose yourself to Satan and the world of deception. Truth will be shown you, but it will be your free will to accept it or reject it. Pray, My children, that you will grow in your love for Me and help others to see the beauty and peace of My love. Pray and prepare, for your time of decision is at hand."

P53 — "My people, I am giving you another message as I gave you once before, that in all likelihood you will see My warning come during the football season of some year."

P111 — "This warning will be a time when all you have done wrong in My eyes will be revealed as such to you. Many have wandered from the faith, or the evil one has lulled you into a spiritual slumber where you do not even recognise sin. With this experience, all will at once know what sin is, without any question. My truth will be revealed to you, and you will see why sin offends Me. Even though some will not think they are sinning, they will now see through the eyes of knowledge what they have done. After, all men will have a true opportunity to come to Me for forgiveness. You will have this one last chance to confess your sins, or face eternal hell fire if you reject Me. The decision will be yours to make. So choose life in My love, or the hate of the evil one."

P184 — "My people, the time is drawing close for My warning. The hour of mercy will be visiting you at the door. See My grace in this vision which will be showered on all the people. The knowledge of good and evil that you have done throughout your life will be made known to you. No longer will you be able to deny My presence. No longer will you be able to admit that you are not a sinner. I, who have seen everything in secret, will show you your faults, and how I envision your soul at this time. For those who wish to reform your lives, you will have the grace of a good confession. But for those who refuse My grace and mercy, you will be choosing your eternal punishment in hell, which you will live to regret."

Hell — a frightening experience. Don't listen to the devil

"Your time of decision will enable you to understand the gravity of this decision. Your whole life's destiny will be determined by whether you accept Me or not. Choose Me and you will have eternal bliss with Me in heaven. Reject Me and you will suffer the pain of never seeing Me again. As well, you will suffer the painful flames of hell for eternity. The experience in hell is so frightening, that you will do well to even come to Me out of fear of this punishment. Do not listen to the devil in the pleasures of this world, for all of this will come to naught. It is your soul's destiny that is your most important concern. I seek you out always, even to the day you die, even more than the devil seeks you, for I have made you and I wish all My creatures to be in My joyous presence."

Prepare to join Jesus before the Warning. A period of grace after the Warning

P223 — "My people ... you must spread My word in all lands, so that every soul has been given a choice between Me and the world. It is better to be prepared to join Me before the warning. There will be a grace period after the warning for repenting, but conversion in that time will be difficult. After this last extension of My mercy, no one will be able to deny My existence or not know of My word. This is when those who choose to be with Me will be immediately tested. You will not be alone at that time, since I and My angels will be there to guide you. This will be the great decision of each life. Choose wisely since you will be choosing your eternal fate."

P259 — "My people, I am preparing you for My warning, but without telling you when. Avoid speculation on this day of mercy. Instead, pray and go to confession often, so you will be found in My grace. Those in serious sin will have dreadful experiences.... remember to pray that sinners may be blessed to return to Me after their life review."

Many will not change but will know their defiance of God

P261 — "My death on the cross was My most precious outflow of mercy to all My human children. Now, in this evil age, you will witness another outpouring of My mercy in My heavenly warning to your souls. It is this spiritual awakening which I will perform for each soul, that will let each of you appraise your life through the eyes of your loving God and Divine Judge. Many will still refuse Me but after the warning they will be more cognisant of their open defiance of My love. Others, out of fear or love, will seek confession to allow Me to forgive their sins. These converts are the souls you must assist in finding Me, and sharing in My forgiveness. By accepting Me as Saviour, you will bring salvation to your house that day."

The Warning — Time for conversion and reparation

P262 — "Now, My people, My merciful warning awaits every soul living in this age. People at death see their life and sins reviewed, but they must expect judgement without being able to change anything. You will be given the glorious opportunity to see your sins, and, in addition, you will be afforded time for conversion and reparation before your judgement. This extension again of My infinite mercy will give every soul one last chance to see their sin and seek My forgiveness. Do not discard this last visitation of My mercy, but take it to heart and be converted through confession, lest you be judged unworthy, and will be cast into the eternal flames of hell."

Volume V — Oct '96 to Dec '96

The Sacrament of Reconciliation — our only hope

P14 — "My people, you are seeing a sign of My warning which is coming soon. I am coming again to prepare My people spiritually for this event. Remember, I have told you that those with serious sin will suffer a more traumatic experience. I come, therefore, to seek your forgiveness of sin in confession. See that My Sacrament of Reconciliation is your only hope to right yourself with Me before this mini-judgement. I am always here, patiently waiting for your return."

Volume VIII — Jul '97 to Sep '97

After the Warning — no middle ground. The choice is for or against God

P76 — "My people, this light [as in the vision] will illuminate your souls as you flash back to all of your days. Each day of your life will be brought before each of you, to show you how I have seen all of your actions. This is an embodiment of the warning experience which all of mankind will come to know. Be prepared to evangelise the lost souls who may for a short time be predisposed to believe in Me. This God, whom some have denied, will be made real to them and they will have to make a decision to be with Me or against Me. There will be no middle ground, as everyone will be forced to choose God or not. This will be a touching moment for many souls and possibly their last chance to be saved. When this event comes upon you, struggle unceasingly to bring back souls to Me."

Nothing is secret from God — all our deeds exposed

P95 — "My people, do not think the evil deeds that you do in secret will go unnoticed. I tell you soon a time of illumination will come upon you. You will see all of your evil deeds exposed before all of heaven like in broad daylight, only brighter. Your sins of crimson red will be shown to you. This warning time is, for some, your last opportunity to realise how evil you have been. Heed this chance and seek forgiveness of your sins. Although your sins be scarlet, I will receive you into conversion. Free yourselves of all of your sinful ways, and come walk in the light of My truth."

Volume XI — Apr '98 to Jun '98

P40 — "My attempts to get your attention have fallen on deaf ears. I will try once again to get your attention through the next wave of storms and pestilence of insects, disease and fires. If you still do not come to your knees, I will send My warning among you to make you realise how your sins offend Me."

A new consciousness — we will see all our life's experiences

P62 — The vision: "…I could see the outline and shadow of a ship at sea. There was a sense that all the people on board came into a different state of conscientiousness (sic)." Jesus said:

P62 — "My people, this vision is what it will be like at the time of the warning. All of these souls recognised that they were in a different state of life than they were used to. It is as if they were suspended in limbo out of time. During this experience, each soul will come face to face with Me as at your judgement. You will see all of your life flashed before you and you will know true right from wrong as I see your actions. You will know how your life stands with Me as if you were to die right now. By a miracle of grace, all of these souls will then return to your original state of life as you know it. You will remember vividly all of your life's experiences to the least detail."

Many will be left in a state of shock

"Now you will be faced with the true condition of your soul as I would see it. Many will be in a state of shock to understand how evil you have been. You will understand more fully about your purpose in life in this place of testing. Some will change their lives and seek forgiveness of their sins. My faithful must be available to lead these souls to Me in confession."

Refusal of some to change — condemnation to hell

"Other souls will convince themselves that this was only an illusion and they will refuse to change their evil ways. These are the souls of those condemned to hell. Pray for these souls for a change of heart or they will be lost. I am revealing this experience to you because the time of My warning draws close. Prepare your souls now with confession, prayer, and fasting and your experience will be less severe than someone in serious sin."

2. The Famine

Volume II — Jul '94 to Jun '95

Have faith and trust in Jesus to provide

P236 — "You will see your food supplies gradually tested by floods and droughts. A famine will be spread over your land and it will be manipulated to force you into the hands of the plans of the evil one. You must have faith and trust in Me that I will provide for you with food and drink. I will provide even manna for those in need to survive this test. Keep faithful to My word and do not listen to or worship anyone else."

Volume IV — Jul to Sep '96

Put aside food and water

P39 — "There is coming a great famine all over the earth. This will be one of the many coming chastisements to purify the earth. Those who do not heed My words, will suffer the ravages of starvation.... Put aside food and water for yourselves. It would be better that all peoples prepare as such, so that looting and stealing of food will not be rampant. This ration will be needed twice. First, before the tribulation, and then during the tribulation when I will provide My manna for you in hiding. I am watching over you by giving you these warnings.

"These food shortages will later fall into the hands of the Antichrist, who will demand allegiance and his mark to buy and sell food in short supply. It is at that time you must flee into hiding with My angel. He will show each of you your way, and provide you with heavenly bread. Listen and heed My words, for your chastisements will be increasing."

Volume VII — Apr to Jun '97

The miracles of food replication

P47 — "My people, many times I have asked you to share your goods with those less fortunate. Now you are seeing a time when you will share your food with the hungry as the famine will spread. This is why it is important to store food now, so you may be able to distribute it later. Do not fear whether you will have enough for others. In the time of the tribulation, I will perform miracles of food replication so all of My faithful will be provided for. It is enough that you prepare the soul spiritually and do not worry about the body's needs. Pray much and I will be helping all of you in your needs."

Volume VIII — Jul '97 to Sep '97

Food shortages a contrived means to control people

P5 — "My people, I have asked you in previous messages to prepare for this evil age by storing up what little food you can. I have shown you how your weather will threaten your food supplies. Now, you are coming to understand even more how Satan's one world people are contriving means to control people through your food. If you follow My instructions to store food, your needs will be provided for."

P10 — "I have given you this message of the coming famine many times, but today understand that even your drinking water will be scarce. This is why I have asked you to store food and water during your time of plenty. As in the time of Joseph, you will again experience a world famine. The Antichrist will use this food shortage to try to control the people through their buying and selling. My faithful have nothing to fear, since as Joseph saved and provided the food, I will provide you with a ration of My heavenly manna at the proper time. Do not succumb to the mark of the Antichrist, but follow My angels to the refuge where My angels will give you Spiritual Communion with the bread of angels."

Multiplication of food for survival

P46 — "Soon many will suffer from this food shortage for many reasons. Getting food to various suppliers will soon become a difficult task. Other forces will take advantage of this problem to have control over the people. You, My friends, do not have to worry.

"I have asked you to be prepared for this coming shortage. I will even multiply what you have for your survival and you will have no need to depend on others. The Antichrist will exploit this situation for his own gain, but he will be thwarted after a short reign."

A massive world depression — third world countries first

P61 — "As the famine and pestilence comes to the world, many will be fighting for goods and food. There will be a massive world depression that will cause national economic systems to falter and some to fail. Many will become so desperate for help to quell the riots and food shortages, that they will accept the man of peace in the Antichrist. He will be allowed to control everyone by their buying and selling with the chip. Many of My faithful will reject him and his so-called help."

P69 — "…you will start to see the effects of poor harvests on your food supplies. The poor people in the third world countries will experience this first. Then, in your turn, you will see the food growing more scarce."

Reliance on food set aside. Roving bands seeking food

"The rich will lord it over the poor and many riots and wars will break out over food shortages. Theft will be rampant before supplies even reach the stores. As less food will be on the stores' shelves, you will have to rely more and more on the food you have set aside. Then roving bands will seek out any food available and many will flee the cities at this time. Have faith, My children, and I will protect you.... Prepare spiritually and physically, for this time will be a great test of your faith in My Words."

Increasing difficulty to buy and sell

P91 — "Food will soon be used as a means to control people. I have told you to prepare for a famine by storing up extra food and water. The ability to buy and sell food will get increasingly difficult until supplies will be limited.... Much chaos will ensue as people become desperate for food. This may bring about the need to go into hiding sooner as stealing and killing for food will be rampant. This is the condition that I have told you will make it ripe for the Antichrist to take control — during a general crisis. This also will be a time of financial unrest all over the world."

Volume XI — Apr to Jun '98

Increasing weather problems

P96 — "My people, you are continuing to witness the drought and heat that are bringing your fires. Storms, droughts and fires will intensify during the next few months. Many of your conveniences and comforts will be endangered by this testing. People will become so upset with these problems, that you will be on your knees praying for rain.... As food supplies dwindle, no longer will people scoff at this possibility."

Volume XIII — Oct to Dec '98

Save one year's supply of food and water

P81 — "My people, I wish to emphasise again your need to save one year's supply of food and water. This is to be done now to prepare for many shortages that will occur before the Antichrist takes over as leader. I will multiply whatever My faithful need, but you must have trust in Me…"

3. Pope John Paul II and The Imposter Pope

Revelation 13: 1- 6

"And I saw a beast rising out of the sea, having ten horns and seven heads; and on its horns were ten diadems, and on its heads were blasphemous names. And the beast that I saw was like a leopard, its feet were like a bear's and its mouth was like a lion's mouth. And the dragon gave it his power and his throne and great authority. One of its heads seemed to have received a death-blow, but its mortal wound had been healed. In amazement the whole earth followed the beast. They worshipped the dragon, for he had given his authority to the beast, and they worshipped the beast, saying, 'Who is like the beast, and who can fight against it?' The beast was given a mouth uttering haughty and blasphemous words, and it was allowed to exercise authority for forty-two months. It opened its mouth to utter blasphemies against God, blaspheming his name and his dwelling, that is, those who dwell in heaven."

Volume I — Jul '93 to Jun '94

Major upheaval and schism in the Church. Exile of the Pope

P25 — "There will be a major upheaval in the Church. Schism will flourish everywhere. This will come about as a result of the Pope issuing his latest encyclical." "The present Pope will go into exile."

P32 — "As more of the tenets of the Pope's recent encyclical become known, there will be more dissension. Some bishops will refuse to follow Rome, causing an upheaval in the Church."

P52 — "The Holy Father is being tested physically and spiritually by some evil clergy around him. They are keeping him from fulfilling his mission to lead the Church in unity. They will try hard to remove him from office either attacking his health or claiming some false scandals.

"By exiling him they hope to replace him with a man called the 'Black Pope' who will be possessed or influenced by the demons. Pray for the Holy Father and the unity of the Church in Me."

Some shepherds like wolves in sheep's clothing

P61 — "Be on guard, My faithful ones, for some of My shepherds are like wolves in sheep's clothing. Some are misleading My people and are conspiring against My son John Paul II.... They do not always follow the Pope but do as they please."

P213 — Mary: "You are blessed to have my Pope son, John Paul II, as your reigning pontiff. He is a holy man and very close to my heart. You must be watchful as the end times approach. He will suffer much for my Jesus. He is steadfast in preserving the Church's teachings. But he will encounter much persecution. I have interceded with my Son to protect him from harm. Do not be surprised if he is exiled and that it may occur on the thirteenth of some month in the future."

Political upheaval in Italy

"There will be a political upheaval at that time in Italy which will precipitate his exile. In his place a false prophet will be installed through the agents of the evil one. These and many events will occur before my triumph will be ushered in by my Son. Pray, my children, and keep close to my Son."

Volume II — Jul '94 to Jun '95

Listen to Pope John Paul II. He is the Pope for these times

P128 — "Listen to My beloved John Paul II. He is My representative on earth, who leads you in faith and morals. Abide by his decisions since the Holy Spirit is working in him. He will lead you well, since I have brought him up especially for your time before the trial. He it is whom I have appointed to prepare you for the tribulation to come. Give thanks for the gift I bring you in his life."

Election of evil pope. He will mislead the people

P230 — "My people, you will soon see some events leading up to My Pope being replaced by a strange election. There will be a power struggle among My prelates and My Pope, John Paul II, may be silenced or exiled. Then they will deliver up a new leader who will eventually usurp power and lead My Church astray for a while. This will lead up to the time of the Antichrist, who will have a new Pope helping him. My Church will be in disarray at that time and will splinter into several factions. Many of My faithful will then suffer persecution for not following the new pope's agenda. You must pray to preserve My remnant Church. Come to Me in hope and trust and I will help you bear up during your future trials."

Volume III — Jul '95 to Jun '96

P80 — "Many Catholics come to see My vicar, but they come in name only, since they do not follow what he teaches. If you would follow Me, then follow the words of My Pope son. He teaches the true position of My Church. Follow him and do not be misled by other false witnesses who have a false interpretation of My Church."

P81 — "Prepare, My people, to hear My word addressed by My Pope. Listen to his words and take them to heart. He is the one now giving you the explanation of My Word. He is calling you in love and peace to be joined with Me in My work of salvation. Be inspired by My Pope, to live each day in the faith I have given you, through My apostles. This faith must endure for all of you, even into the time of tribulation."

The imposter pope will follow the Antichrist. Do not believe him

P116 — "My people, I have honoured your prayers, and have done My mother's bidding in protecting My Pope son from Satan's hand. The evil one's time is almost at hand. It will soon be time for My chosen one to be forced out of office. There will be a great election and an evil pope will come forth. All manner of blasphemy and contradiction will come from this black pope, and Satan will then cause a schism in My Church. It will be at this time, that My faithful remnant will be split away from those willing to follow the worldly ways of the black pope. The evil pope will be cunning and powerful in misleading the people. Do not follow his decrees, but follow only those things taught by the old fathers of My Church. Your faith will indeed be tested, but follow My warning and gather separately in your prayer groups, where you will find Me in consolation. Pray for My help and I will lead you to what you have to do. Have faith in Me and your reward will be found in heaven."

Beware of the imposter pope. He will be full of deception

P296 — "My people, I am showing you how My Mother and the angels are protecting My Pope son. You will see, as the tribulation comes, that My Pope son will be exiled, as there will be a split in the Church.

An imposter pope will be chosen, but he will be in league with the Antichrist. You will see him relax the Church's positions on the sins of the flesh to accommodate the people's minds and lead them astray. People will be drawn to him, since they will think he is helping them. Gradually, more heresies will come forth as his evil ways will be made known. Since his charisma will draw many away from My laws, I will send St. Michael to smite him. When this antipope takes office, do not believe in what he teaches, for evil will control his heart. Have faith in Me, and I ask My remnant to support Pope John Paul II, even in his exile."

Remain faithful to the Church established by the Apostles

P310 — "You must pray for guidance, My faithful, for soon you will see a schism in My Church. My faithful remnant, who follow the current Pope, will have to go into exile. Continue to follow and keep faithful to the teachings of My Church, established by My apostles. Do not be misled by the apostasy and heresies of the imposter pope. The evil forces are behind this schism, but be prepared so you can follow those priests loyal to Pope John Paul II. Preserve your holy missals and books of the old Mass, since the apostates will change the words dramatically. Take courage, My people, for I will be with you helping you through all of these trials."

Volume IV — Jul to Sep '96

Mary will watch over him as he leads the remnant Church

P36 — "My mother will watch over him as he will lead the remnant Church after the schism in the Church. The Pope's destruction will be sought, but these men will not be able to kill him.… You will see this replacement of the Pope, called the little horn of the Apocalypse [see also Daniel 7: 7-25], bring apostasy and blasphemy to My Church. He will misdirect even some of the elect.

"Remain faithful to My teachings of the faith and reverence John Paul II as My true Pope for this age.… In everything, follow My Word from the Scriptures and do not be misled by bishops and priests who teach heresies as dogma. Pray for My help and I will give discernment to all who ask it of Me."

Volume V — Oct to Dec '96

The imposter pope will violate Church traditions and Dogmas

P15 — "My people, you are seeing men in the Church who would like to take over the papacy, and lead the faithful their own way. They will seize on any opportunity, such as the Pope's health or his age. Satan is directing their ambitions and will use them to mislead the people.

"When you see their pronouncements in conflict with My revealed Scripture, you will see how this is an evil lot that strives for power on an earthly plane. I will gift you with discernment to see how evil these people really are. This new pope, who will replace Pope John Paul II, will be deceptive and lead the people as a tyrant. He will be trying to use his office to promote the Antichrist. Once you recognise the evil in him, you will remember My words, how he will utter abominations and blasphemies.

"Be watchful, for soon you will see his election in violation of the proper succession of popes. This imposter is not to be obeyed, but reject him, since he will be in league with the Antichrist. Pray for My help to discern."

Volume VI — Jan to Mar '97

Revolt of bishops and cardinals. Do not be deceived

P30 — "My people, My bishops and cardinals are in revolt. They honour the Holy Father with their lips, but their hearts are far from Me. Some of My own leaders are harboring thoughts of how to exile My Pope son, and install one of their own leaders. This newly elected pope will give them what they want, but it will come at the cost of a schism in My Church. This new pope will have evil roots and will mislead many away from Me, as he will declare many heresies valid.

"Do not be deceived by this imposter pope, who will be very subtle at first, but gradually will accept the leadership of the Antichrist. This first beast comes with lies and deceits that will even persuade some of My elect. Refuse all of his teachings and hold fast to the teachings I have given My apostles. I will watch over you if you seek Me to help you in this tribulation."

Follow only Pope John Paul II as successor to the Apostles

P30 — "My people, I have sent you My Pope son as a special grace, especially for this time. I ask you to follow him and listen to all of his decrees and writings. He is the one to teach you faith and morals as given to you from My apostles. This is the line of succession of St Peter that I have promised to protect My Church."

P52 — "There will indeed be a special election controlled by the evil element of the cardinals. **My Pope son will be forced out of office and the new false witness will bring a schism into My Church.** I am telling you My people to follow My traditional teachings and do not listen to the misguiding imposter pope."

P81 — "My people, I am showing you once again how My Pope John Paul II, will be exiled by a new pope who will assume power ... Pope John Paul II will lead My remnant Church. Look to the fruits of this new pope, for you will see him violate long standing traditions and dogmas. Eventually, he will even endorse the Antichrist and you will know how evil he will be in all his subtle ways. He is the one who will be slain, but he will rise again from the Antichrist's power [Rev.13:3]. The two beasts will reign but a moment in time, then I will strike them down and My victory will be witnessed. This is the long awaited victory over evil when Satan and the beasts will be chained in hell while My era of peace endures."

Volume VII — Apr to Jun '97

Preserve the teachings of the Church, as given by the apostles

P25 — "I have asked you many times to preserve My teachings and commands handed down by the apostles. In your eagerness to reform do not discard any of the foundations of My Church. Follow the teachings of My Pope-son John Paul II and you will be following the teaching authority of My Church."

Volume X — Jan to Mar '98

P9 — Mary: "My dear children, pray for your Vicar of Christ in your Pope John Paul II. He is being tested by those around him and by his health. Your prayers can strengthen him in his daily work. If you do not support him, he will fall easily into the hands of his persecutors. Give him your allegiance and support his teachings even if they be unpopular with your clergy."

P27 — "My people, I am calling My apostles in the readings today, and My Pope son, John Paul II is following in the steps of St. Peter. Look to him as your shepherd…"

Pray for Pope John Paul II — the last faithful Pope before Antichrist

P41 — "My people, this Pope of Mine, you have now, you need to cherish and protect. He is My last faithful Pope before the Antichrist and the antipope dominate the scene. They will bring up charges and criticisms of John Paul II so they can elect this evil pope, who will reign next. **Pray much for John Paul II for he will be leading My remnant Church.**"

P66 — "My people, I am showing you how My Pope son, John Paul II, is leading My flock to heaven. Listen to him in every decree and instruction and make it a part of your life. Never doubt My power that I will watch over My Church, even during the tribulation. The Church is led by My Pope John Paul II, and do not listen to any other who claims to be Me."

Volume XI — Apr to Jun '98

All will have to chose either John Paul II or the imposter

P20 — "My people, I am again showing you this coming split in My Church, indicated by the two pulpits. You will be forced to choose between the church of the antipope or the church of My remnant which is led by Pope John Paul II. Those who follow the antipope will be defying the laws and traditions set up by the apostles.... I have given you many messages concerning this schism in My Church, because it will be very subtle and will confuse many. **See when Pope John Paul II leaves Rome or is claimed dead, that the schism will begin**. This is the warning to go into hiding, since the Antichrist will soon take power and imprison and kill all those against the New World Order."

P49 — "My people, there will be a great celebration in the Church before the coming of the Antichrist. **Many will be cheering your current Pope for awhile**. Then evil will prevail over Rome for a short time. It will be My triumph later that will usher in My renewed earth when all My faithful will rejoice in My love. My victory will be so overwhelming that no one will ever doubt My power is complete."

Volume XIII — Oct to Dec '98

Illegal election of new pope and exile of Pope John Paul II. Underground Masses will be necessary.

P23 — "My people, I am preparing you for the time when a schism will occur in My Church.... The next elected pope **will occur while My Pope son, John Paul II will still be alive**. My Pope son will be exiled and an evil pope will assume his position. He will change the Mass and many laws with his decrees, but they will violate My tradition and the faith passed on by My apostles. Pray for discernment."

P46 — "When My Pope son John Paul II leaves Rome in exile, **you are to go into hiding under the direction of your guardian angels** to holy-ground refuges, or the caves."

P64 — "My people, I have told you **that an evil man will illegally be elected pope** and he will control all the Churches. He will eventually try to force My faithful to worship the Antichrist, even in My Churches. That is why My remnant will leave the churches under his control and go to underground Masses in their homes and other secret places.

"This Antipope will even try to mislead My Church into taking the Mark of the Beast. The image of the beast will be the new god placed on these altars. I am telling you now, My people, NOT to obey and follow this evil pope, because he will lead you only to hell, in following the Deceiver in the Antichrist. Pray for discernment to see the evil ways of both the antipope and the Antichrist."

This imposter pope is the "false witness" spoken of in the Book of Revelation (Rev. 16:13, 19:20).

"Do not be taken in by his scholarly wisdom, but see the evil fruits of his deeds. When there is a lack of love and a coldness in his heart, you will recognise the evil in both the antipope and the Antichrist. Avoid their influence by hiding and do *not* follow any of their commands. Follow only Me, and I will sustain you through this trial. By My love and only through Me will anyone be saved."

4. The Mark of the Beast — The Chip

Revelation 13: 15-18

"And it was allowed to give breath to the image of the beast so that the image of the beast could even speak and cause those who would not worship the image of the beast to be killed. Also it causes all, both small and great, both rich and poor, both free and slave, to be marked on the right hand or the forehead, so that no one can buy or sell who does not have the mark, that is the name of the beast or the number of its name. This calls for wisdom: let anyone with understanding

*calculate the number of the beast, for it is the number
of a person. Its number is six hundred and sixty-six."*

Volume II - Jul '94 to Jun '95

Refuse the Mark even under pain of death — trust in Jesus

P50 — "You will soon see a call for all people to receive this computer chip so they can be registered with the world computer, the "Beast". This will be hailed as a means for more efficient buying and selling but in actuality it will be the Antichrist's means to control people. This is the mark of the beast you should avoid at all costs. Refuse this even under pain of death or you will not be written in the Book of Life. It will be at this time you will need a heavy trust in Me to take care of you. The warning will come before any transition of power so you will truly know that you will be choosing either Me or Satan."

P218 — "I am telling you as before not to take the mark of the beast even though you may not be able to buy and sell. If you take this mark, you will know that with it you will be asked to praise the Antichrist and not Me. **If you knowingly give in to this, you will be in the book of the living dead** and not in My Book of Life. You cannot be with Me and still belong to the world."

Volume III — Jul '95 to Jun '96

The hypnotic state of those with the chip

P235 — "My people, this vision shows you how the Antichrist and his agents will control the people. Those, who against My will, have taken the mark of the beast, initially, for buying and selling, will see themselves controlled as well. At the time directed by these agents, they will summon the people and force them to worship the Antichrist at services. **By passing this light beam among those with the chip, it will excite the chip, and bring these people under a hypnotic state.** These people will be drawn to worship the Antichrist as often as the agents desire. These people will follow the agents' wishes to perform whatever they want. This is another reason to enforce My wish, that you avoid this mark of the beast, or you will be lost."

Smart cards with the chip — reject these even if you cannot buy or sell

P268 — "Soon you will be encouraged to take smart cards, carrying computer chips, as your credit cards. This is the stage that you must reject taking the smart card, for it is the beginning of the groundwork for the mark of the beast. From this card, they will soon offer something as watches with these chips, so they can just scan your hand. There will be great publicity then, [on] how vulnerable people are to theft of their smart cards. It is at this point that they will offer to place chips in the hand for security purposes. Little by little, this will become the only accepted means to buy and sell at the stores. Gradually, everyone will be encouraged to take this chip in the hand. It is then that you should leave for hiding, since the next stage will be to force everyone to take the chip.

"Those who refuse to take the chip will be outlaws, and not able to buy and sell. At this time, the Antichrist will soon come and use this device to control his people. Remember, do not take the chip in the hand or you will be lost forever. I am warning you now, not even to take the smart cards. **No one with this chip will be written in the Book of Life.**"

Volume IV — Jul '96 to Sep '96

Antichrist unable to find those who don't take the chip

P40 — "My people, I am showing you how the Antichrist will control people who have the mark of the beast. He will call a meeting, and those with the chip will be summoned and controlled to listen to his suggestions and his brainwashing. It is important to realise that the Antichrist will not be able to find you if you do not take this chip. If you wish to be saved, you must trust in Me and reject the chip, even if it means death or torture. Believe in My words of hope and protection, for I will be your only alternative to Satan."

Volume VI — Jan '97 to Mar '97

Need to go into hiding to avoid detention centres

P33 — "The one world people will subtly bring the chip to the public, encouraging them of its advantages. Then they will try to force you to take the chip. This is where the detention centres and the helicopters will be used for crowd control, for the dissenters who do not want to take the chip. Soon you will have to go into hiding as I have told you. All of these messages are coming to an open understanding of these events.

"Remember never take the chip in your hand or forehead or you will be lost. Those who think they can remove it will be deceived, since the Antichrist will then control you. As soon as the chips have been placed in the people, the Antichrist will take control over all nations."

Volume VII — Apr '97 to Jun '97

Antichrist declaration when satellites and chips in place

P40 — "My people, you must be aware that the campaign to place the mark of the beast in all people will be soon under way. Once the one world bankers have employed the smart cards and readers throughout the world, they will be ready to use the mark of the beast in the hand. This transition from the smart card to the chip in the hand will be very swift, since everything will be in place from the smart cards. Once the satellites and the chips are in place, the Antichrist will declare himself in a world takeover. At that time his power will be most strong and you are to be in hiding, so he cannot force you to worship him. Events leading up to this power struggle will be very subtle and quick. You will be misled into a peaceful state of mind and your media will keep the total truth from everyone."

Three signs of when to go into hiding

Look to the signs of [1] the warning, [2] My Pope's exile and [3] this mark of the beast to know when to go into hiding. When you see these events, do not hesitate to go or you may risk being captured and attempts will be made to force you to worship the Antichrist. Fear not, for I will be with you."

Don't be deceived by advertising for the chip in the hand

P60 — "The advances in this technology are moving fast, since evil's time is running out. These evil people will claim how easy these chips are to use and they are more secure embedded in your hand.... What they will not tell you, is how these chips will become the only way to buy and sell.... If you are found refusing the chip, they will place you in detention centres ringed with fences. You will be prisoners and tortured or martyred. Come to me, therefore, and seek My help. For without My help, you will surely be lost ... Guard your souls now, lest Satan steal it away."

Low orbit communications satellites — monitoring of every move

P78 — "My people, you should be aware how important it is to know all about these low orbit communications satellites. These satellites will be periodically scanning various sectors for people that have the chip in their smart card or in the hand. The one world people will monitor your every move to get a profile on whether you are abiding by their laws. They will be searching soon on the ground to make sure everyone has a smart card. This is why I have asked you not to take the smart card or the chip in the hand."

Restrictions on travel, jobs, buying and selling

"You eventually will be forced to worship the Antichrist through these chips in order to buy and sell. You will not be able to drive your car, cross state or national lines or hold a job without a smart card. This is why these satellites are so significant, since they will be what allows the Antichrist to control people all over the world. This evil reign will be world wide but cannot last against My power.... Pray for My triumph to come soon so all of Satan's forces will be denied the souls that they wish to possess."

Satan's deception — don't be misled by claims to peace

P84 — "My people, through all the mist of deception given out by Satan, do not be misled by his powers to bring a so-called peace to the earth. These men, I have shown you before, [in the vision] are preparing the countries to accept the mark of the beast. They are subtly bringing about mass usage of the smart card chips. They will try and implement this chip so all will use it to buy and sell. See in your time before the Antichrist comes, his agents are preparing the people so they will be under his control."

Be prepared to die rather than take the chip — Jesus will provide if we trust in Him

"All of these messages are given as a warning not to have anything to do with this mark of the beast. Even if you must die to avoid this chip, continue to worship Me only and never give allegiance to anyone else. By not taking the mark of the beast or its forerunner in the smart card, you will be forced to flee your homes and your jobs. The Antichrist **and his agents will try to force this mark on everyone. I will provide your shelter, your food and your spiritual protection. Trust in Me** for My help and I will lead you to a land of milk and honey in My new era after My triumph over Satan."

5. The Antichrist

Matthew 24: 15-28 (see also Revelation 13)

"So when you see the desolating sacrifice standing in the holy place, as was spoken by the prophet Daniel, (let the reader understand), [see Daniel 7, 8: 11-14, 9: 27, 12:10-12] then those in Judea must flee to the mountains.... Pray that your flight may not be in winter or on a sabbath. For at that time there will be great suffering, such as has not been from the beginning of the world, no, and never will be. And if those days had not been cut short, no one would be saved; but for the sake of the elect those days will be cut short. Then if anyone says to you, 'Look, here is the Messiah!' or 'there he is' — do not believe it. For false messiahs and great prophets will appear and produce great signs and omens, to lead astray, if possible, even the elect. Take note, I have told you beforehand. So, if they say to you, 'Look! He is in the wilderness,' do not go out. If they say, 'Look! He is in the inner rooms,' do not believe it. For as the lightning comes from the east and flashes as far as the west, so will be the coming of the Son of Man. Wherever the corpse is, there the vultures will gather."

Volume I — Jul '93 to Jun '94

P19 — "The Antichrist will come from Egypt (much like Jesus came out of Egypt). He will bring a false peace during an upheaval in the world. Prepare for the Antichrist — he will win many away from God."

Control of Minds. Demonic powers

P29 — "The Antichrist will have eyes which you should avoid. He will be able to hypnotise your thoughts and gain control of your mind. He will have demonic powers and you should hide from him. He and the men he will influence will seek out the faithful and try not only to kill the body but to steal the soul from God if they are not protected."

Conjunction of Stars

P36 — "It will be an evil age when all will seem lost. But be faithful and keep in hiding for your salvation is near."

"There will be a conjunction of stars as at the star of Bethlehem. Only this time it will be a sign of the Antichrist coming to power. It will be visible to those on the ground and the astronomers will witness it to the people. From that moment, the demons will be loosed to roam the earth and they will trouble men's souls. Evil will increase in men as a result and the faithful will be tested severely. At that time, you will understand all My warnings and prayer will be necessary to save your soul."

The mark on the forehead — recognition of God's people

P44 — "During the future evil times you will need to pray to Me for discernment that you can recognise faithful Christians apart from the evil impersonators. You will recognise your own with the mark on their foreheads — God's own elect. The others with the mark of the beast should be shunned, for at that time they will be lost and a spiritual threat to you. Pray and be on the watch."

Underground Masses. Rosaries our only weapon

P45 — "...the demons will grow in strength and eventually force the churches to close. At that time you may have underground

Masses for a while, until the priests are also found. In the end of the evil age you will huddle together to say your rosaries — this will be your only weapon against evil. This time will be short and My Kingdom will soon come in full glory for you to share."

Events will speed up. Protection of houses of prayer

P46 — "Events will be speeded up dramatically as the demons take power. Because of My people's sin and lack of prayer, there will be many chastisements sent to your land. You will be tested such that it will seem like a raging inferno. **Those houses where prayer is said constantly, I will protect from the flames — but woe to those houses that do not pray.** The fires now in the west will be pale in comparison to what will be coming. Some of this can be mitigated by prayer but not all. Start as many prayer groups as possible to stem the tide of the coming evil — for it will exact My justice. I love My people always and am waiting for your love, but the lukewarm I detest."

Evil bishops and cardinals. Exile of Pope John Paul II

P47 — "A demon-possessed bishop will gain power over the cardinals and will exile My son John Paul II. This will cause strife in My Church but keep courage."

P52 — "There are evil intended bishops and cardinals already infiltrated into My Church. They are the ones influenced by demons who are sowing the seeds of dissension. There will as a result be many rifts among the clergy in defilement of the unity I desire for My Church. I urge you to pray for your priests and bishops that they will not go astray."

A Time of Chaos. Entrance of the Antichrist

P163 — "You will see a time where events will seem like they are happening almost simultaneously. Time will appear as if it was speeded up. A time of chaos throughout the world will occur. All these events will cause people to demand some stable leadership. These things will make way for the entrance of the Antichrist. He will appear as a man of peace with great powers but his reign will not last long.

"Fear not, I will be with you to protect you in those times. But know that if the events were not speeded up, even the endurance of the faithful would be tried. I am always in control and My Mother's triumph will soon be upon you after this time. Pray and ask My help during these coming battles against evil."

P169 — "During the evil time of darkness there will be many demonic spirits roaming the earth seeking souls to claim for their own.... This time will be as the Passover was for the Jews. I will protect My faithful from the demon clutches with holy sacramentals such as crosses and the rosary. The devil will claim those who deny Me by following their own lust for the things of this world. For those who have put other gods before Me, this will be their judgement to hell. They will indeed be tortured by the demons.... My Mother's triumph will reign for a millennium."

Need to pray for discernment. Form prayer Groups

P175 — "Pray for discernment from the Holy Spirit on any issue you are unsure of and live your life in My peace."

P177 — "Prepare! Prepare! Prepare! The time of evil days will soon be upon you. You must pray constantly and keep close to My power for you are seeing the beginning of the great apostasy. My churches will either be closed by the government or slowly taken over by those teaching a humanistic religion devoid of Me. My remnant Church will be forced into their houses to meet as My community. This is why your prayer groups are necessary to keep close together."

Seek out underground Masses to avoid heretical teachings

P182 — "You will at first have to seek out underground Masses to avoid the heretical teachings. Then there will be confrontations, and they will try to ban you from your churches for believing in My true faith. The people of this time will allow the demons to cause them all perversions of sex and drugs. It will be much like Sodom and Gomorrah in Lot's time. This is why My judgement must come again with fire to purify the earth. It will be so perverted that it will require My intervention to bring peace once again to the earth. There will only be a small remnant left to preach My true Gospel."

Antichrist — appearance of a peacemaker. A tyrannical ruler, intent on destruction

P194 – "All those means of world control will lead to his coming into power. He will thrive on control of the trade, food and the finances. The horrible scenes as in Africa will continue to get out of hand prompted by the evil one. As chaos drags on, people will call for a leader to stop the killings. This is how he will come to reign — by claiming to bring peace to the world. Once in power though, he will use his tyranny to persecute My faithful elect. This religious persecution will seem hopeless but I tell you it will not last but an inkling of time. For I will bring swift justice to this evil lot and they will all be cast into the fiery abyss of hell never to threaten My elect again. Then My era of peace and grace will be with you.... Continue to have trust in Me and My words of Scripture. I will not let you down for anything you ask for in My name."

P226 — "I tell you many people will be drawn to him as he may deceive even some of My faithful. They will carry him off to be their ruler. But his kingdom will be of short duration. Do not be taken in by his cunning and seeming miracles. His real intent is to destroy and consume as many souls as will accept him. But you are to remain faithful to the one true God."

Volume II — Jul '94 to Jun '95

The need to flee the cities — torture and martyrdom

P15 — "The days of the tribulation are almost upon you. Know that I have gone before you and have suffered pain and death for you. Some of My faithful also will be tested with torture and martyrdom. I tell you to flee the cities if you want to spare your lives, for the evil one will dominate the people most in the cities. Thus far you have seen evil inspired men, but you are yet to see evil incarnate as will happen in the end times. This evil will require My help and your guardian angels to protect your souls from the demons.

"You must have full faith and trust in Me to weather this battle of good and evil. Those who endure it though, will receive a reward, even while still on earth, as I come in glory to purify this evil."

Prayer groups. Jesus' cross our protection — wear it

P19 — "You will find strength spiritually and much consolation in your prayer groups, for where two or three are gathered, I am in their midst. With My help you will overcome evil and no longer fear it, for when you have Me, you have everything."

"My cross is the symbol of your salvation. It keeps showing you how much I love you that I would die for you. Keep My likeness in the cross in your house and a crucifix [with the body on it] on your person. It will be a protection for you during the evil times."

Arrival of Antichrist after the Warning. Pray constantly

P30 — "After this event [the warning] you will see the entrance of the Antichrist as he will come to power.... Do not fear this time, but rejoice in your suffering for you will soon see My glory come upon the earth as Satan will be vanquished in all his attempts to harm man. My people, you must continue in constant prayer to ask My help to endure this time."

Antichrist — use of technology, TV, virtual reality

P43 — "...the Antichrist will use all the technology available to his advantage via the TV. He will come to power and most of the people will give him homage, except My faithful remnant. You will be protected from his wiles as I have promised you...."

P45 — "The Antichrist will exploit the use of virtual reality over the TV using it for mind control with earthly "high" feelings. As I have told you, avoid this on your TV and probably get rid of them at that time for they will only be serving evil purposes... I am asking you to say the St. Michael prayer often for his help to fight the demons."

P75 — "My people, during the tribulation you will see many give praise and honour to the Antichrist. They will treat him as a god because of his miraculous powers. [See Revelation 13: 13-14].They will make sacrifices to him even, possibly, human sacrifices as they do even now in hidden places."

Help of St. Michael

P85 — St. Michael the Archangel — "I stand before God the most powerful angel in heaven. The Lord has given me to guard over

His people from Lucifer and his angels. I have heard many prayers to me and I stand by watching over the Church and all who invoke Me. I am ever at your service to provide for the Lord's faithful. Call on me often when you are threatened by evil or if the evil angels are about. During the tribulation you will need me most when all the angels in hell will be allowed to roam the earth."

The two beasts — The false pope and the Antichrist — See Rev. 13

P86 — "You will need an abundance of My help and you will need to call on your guardian angels to protect you from the powers of evil. Do not seek to follow them even out of curiosity, but avoid their influence at all costs. They will be much more powerful than humans. This is why you should hide from their powers of suggestion and persuasion.... I will protect you physically and spiritually. Have faith in Me and you will see My promises come true."

Do not take up arms

P91 — "Remember how I reprimanded Peter when he used his sword. Do not take up arms in these evil days. The devil wants you to fight each other over anything. Give up what you have rather than fight, for I will provide for your needs."

False Prophets — Discern all very carefully

P91 — "Do not be fooled by the many false prophets who will come in My name. Discern very carefully each person's message to determine if it is of God. For by their fruits you will know them. If they do not lead proper lives according to My law, this will cast doubt upon their ministry. If they teach things contrary to the Gospels, know again their false ways.

"You must be clever as foxes to know who is with Me and who is against Me. If such people are very proud and boasting of themselves or worldly, know also this is not in conformity with a man of God. Trust only those who are humble and trying to follow My will, for this is what I ask of all My disciples."

Signs and wonders will announce the Antichrist — an eclipse

P97 — "I have told you before you will see many signs and wonders to announce both the beginning reign of Antichrist and

My Second Coming shortly after. Know that an eclipse will usher in the evil age of darkness. At that time, you should be in hiding to avoid the powers of darkness. Many will be persecuted in various ways, even some will face martyrdom. Pray for the strength of My help and your guardian angel to get you through these days. Life will be hard for a while, but your experience in My reign of peace will more than make up for it. Have faith and hope that I will protect your soul."

P99 — "...know you will be either with Me or against Me. There will be no middle ground. No longer can you put off to tomorrow your decision. Since once you take the mark of the beast, you will have fallen into his clutches never to be with Me again."

Pink Lightning — power of Antichrist

P114 — "When you see this phenomenon of pink lightning, know that it is the time of the Antichrist. He will call this form of lightning to the ground as if bringing fire out of the sky [See Revelation 13: 11-18]. This will so mesmerise some with his power that he will convert many non-believers to his side. His wonders and powers will be a new reign of principalities and powers which will overcome those souls who are weak and not full of My grace. He will lead them as a Pied Piper to a deception of his lies such that they will do everything he says."

Persecution — build up spiritual strength now

"They will even seek out Christians for him to persecute. They will be acting as robots under his complete control. This is why I tell you, My people, to build up your spiritual strength now since the evil one will test even My elect to the breaking point. But reach out to Me, My children, and I will protect you. Have faith in Me always no matter what the odds, and you will have a peace which no other creature can give you."

Be prepared for Jesus' Second Coming. Pray and fast now

P124 — "My people, I have warned you many times to be prepared for My Second Coming. As I look out over My people, most of you have not taken Me very seriously on My request. If you do not ready yourself with your spiritual armour for the test,

Satan will sift you like wheat when the Antichrist comes. You are in the midst of a battle of good and evil whether you want to believe it or not. Read My signs and that of the world and you will see evil is having its day. But pray and fast now at this acceptable time to be saved. For if you approach the end times with a lackadaisical spirit, you will not be ready to fight your adversary. It will only be through My help and grace that you will save your soul. So stay close to Me for your spiritual survival."

Unheard of displays of power — seek help of our guardian angels

P136 — "Woe to you all of earth's inhabitants for an evil time is approaching when there will be previously unheard of displays of power. This is the same time I have told you, if time were not shortened, even My elect would be at risk. You will be fighting principalities and powers from below. You must pray to Me for strength to repel these attacks and have plenty of holy water and your guardian angels to ward off these demons. They are seeking only souls to destroy. They will use all manner of deception to achieve this end. Be prepared with your holy weapons of the rosary and My holy objects as blessed palms or scapulars."

Volume IV — Jul '96 to Sep '96

Those who knowingly take the mark of the beast

P54 — "My people, I am showing you how the mark of the beast will be implanted in people's right hand. This is the chip I have told you to avoid at all costs, even if it will prevent you from buying food. Those who take the mark of the beast knowingly, and are not forced, will be lost to Satan's control. I will provide your food, so do not take this device under any condition."

Antichrist — miraculous powers. The devil incarnate

P64 — "My dear people, it is important that you be prepared to know the powers and plans of the Antichrist. He will be the most evil man to come to earth. He will have miraculous powers, since he will be like a devil incarnate. He must be avoided at all costs, because of his hypnotic power over people, and his charisma to attract followers. His evil will be very subtle at first as he plays the part of a peacemaker. He will be very clever and a father of lies. People will believe his promises and will be drawn into his web of evil. He will seek out souls by buying them with this world's goods, if they would only worship him. **Avoid all electrical communication, since he will have power over the people on TV and the Internet.** Because I have warned you beforehand, realise My words are true, and when you see them fulfilled, do follow Me for safety. I will protect you from all evil, if you pray for My help."

Volume V — Oct '96 to Dec '96

Antichrist's agents — identification of Christians for elimination

P22 — "My people, I wish to give you a serious warning to all who love Me and are faithful to My word. At the coming of the tribulation, the Antichrist's agents will be preparing the way by identifying all those who are Christians, or those who would defy his takeover. When his time comes, you will see his people gather all of those targeted for elimination very quickly. They will be sent to death camps as in previous wars to be tortured or exterminated. It is important, My people, to be on the watch at this time for the beginning of the tribulation, to know when you will be sought out. I will give you a warning when to go into hiding before these agents can capture you. Pray for My guidance and help at this time, since many lives will be taken in this first stage."

Seek Jesus' mercy and help to survive

P25 — "My people, when you see the Antichrist come, do not be taken in by his signs and appearing miracles. He is the father of lies and illusions. Do not listen to him in any way. Instead, hide from him in any way possible, for his influence will challenge even the elect. Seek My mercy and help during this trial, for I will be your only way to be saved. You will not survive spiritually or physically on your own, but with Me, you will be protected."

Antichrist — search by satellites and helicopters. Pray

P31 — "My people, you are seeing how you must flee the Antichrist's agents to avoid being placed in detention centres. I am reminding you that they will search for you with satellites and helicopters, using many electrical sensing devices. You must pray to Me and your angels that we will block their finding you. Those who are faithful to Me, I will protect from all of these demonic forces. You will see My power will overshadow anything that Satan will devise."

Jesus' miracles to protect the faithful

"Even though you think it impossible to avoid these evil forces, I will perform miracles to protect you. Take hope, My children, I will be watching you in spiritual and physical matters. Even amidst evil men, I will thwart their designs on you. I will only allow those intended by My Will to be martyred. The rest will be miraculously cared for. You will not have seen such open protection, since the days I helped My people in the Exodus. This purification time will be shown to be a battle of good and evil that has been destined for centuries."

Another sign of the Antichrist — blue light in the sky

P55 — **The Vision:** *I could see a bright blue light and it seemed to descend upon the earth. After, I saw many snow storms as the weather got colder. Jesus said:* "This will be the peak of Satan's reign in this man called the Antichrist. This blue light in the sky is another sign for his coming to earth in his public life. When you see the increased cold, this represents many souls' hearts will turn cold to Me as well. A call is going out for more prayer at this time to help defend My elect from this trauma of evil. Your consolation is that I will not allow his reign to last long. Time will speed up and I will conquer all evil with one stroke of My hand."

Crowd control — These things not told to frighten people

P93 — "My people, do not be surprised that the evil one will use all available technology for his mission. Many helicopters being placed in position for crowd control near all the big cities. You will see, My children, how ruthless the evil ones can be when they decide to seek global control. These people will ready everyone to be under the control of Antichrist. What you have seen up to now, will pale in the face of these evil forces soon to take over your countries and your cities. These things are being told you, not to frighten the people, but they are being shown to you, so you know what you will be dealing with in preparation for the tribulation."

Those who refuse to prepare

"I keep telling you, that no one will survive without My help.... Those who refuse to prepare for this battle with evil will be found wanting and unprepared. It would be better for you to be spiritually prepared, since you will need all of your spiritual weapons, as the rosary, to fight this battle. Continue to warn the people of these physical traumas, but most of all prepare to guard your souls which are the most valuable."

Volume VII — Apr '97 to Jun '97

P3 — "My people, I have warned you of the coming of the Antichrist as indicated by signs in the sky. What you are seeing now will pale in the face of the miracles he will appear to perform. There will be many illusions of lights in the sky and false signs to declare him as the Christ. Do not worship this man no matter what he says or does."

Unusual light sources — illusion of miraculous powers

P7 — "He will use helicopters and unusual light sources to portray images so that people will think he has miraculous powers. Many of his signs and wonders will be illusions, but still he will have powers of suggestion to mislead the people... he will become a tyrannical leader."

Antichrist's declaration — power in literature and pictures

P76 — "My people, as the time for Antichrist's declaration comes, he will gain in power and all literature or pictures about him will take on more power as well.... do not have any of the Antichrist's writings or pictures around you."

Lasers — for special effects

P77 — "My people, you have heard in the Scriptures [Rev. 13: 13-14] how the Antichrist will be able to call down fire from the heavens... [he]... will use lasers and special effects to try to dazzle people with his powers. He will use illusions and technology as a master magician to influence people. Do not be afraid, My power will suppress him quickly."

Volume VIII — Jul '97 to Sep '97

Churches destroyed in persecution. Even some of the elect will be mislead

P62 — "My people, many of My Churches will be destroyed or abandoned as the Antichrist will persecute My Church. My faithful remnant will be split from the side of the Church that refuses to follow My traditions and the Ten Commandments. This schism in My Church will drive My faithful to an underground Church. Those in control of the schismatic church will mislead even some of the elect. To avoid the powers of the Antichrist and his desire to kill My faithful, you will have to seek hiding in caves as in previous persecutions."

Establish prayer groups. Those refusing Jesus' help may be lost

"Reach out now to establish your prayer groups, where you will find My strength. It is important to convert souls before it may be too late. Once the Antichrist establishes his reign, you will only survive spiritually through My help. Those that refuse to seek My help at that time, will surely be lost."

Volume IX — Oct '97 to Dec '97

Antichrist declaration. Cables, TV, faxes, computers, copiers etc

P61 — "My people, I wish to warn you about the coming of the Antichrist and his declaration time. At the time of his first announcement about his coming in declaration, have all of your cables out of your house and do not watch your television any longer — disconnect them. As it comes closer to the day of his declaration, do away with your telephone lines, your computers, faxes, copiers, radios, and anything electronic that can be influenced by the demons, since they will use them to distract you. In addition to these, stop your newspaper and even your mail. All of these will be controlled."

When to go into hiding. No credit card, smart cards or those with the chip

"Remember, when you see [1] My warning, [2] Pope John Paul II leaving Rome, and [3] the placement of the chips in the hand, you are to pack your sacramentals and your physical needs, ready to go into hiding. Do not have any credit cards, smart cards, nor anyone with the chip in their body, since you can be tracked by these devices. Pray much during this trial for My help and I will instruct your angels where to take you for spiritual safety. This is a time to follow My instruction for helping to save your soul and those of your loved ones and friends."

Volume X — Jan '98 to Mar '98

The Tribulation. Antichrist's declaration — announcement imminent.

P47 — "My people, this sounding gong [as in the vision] is a sign to you that the time of the great tribulation is about to begin. It is so close that you can almost sense its coming. All the signs of this time are already evident. Events of your weather and the rumours of war are all converging to the time when the Antichrist will be announced. You will see events falling one right after the other and if war breaks out, it could move faster. Once the world chaos reaches a fever pitch, it will be the time for the evil one's entrance to his public declaration. You will need much prayer and fasting to endure this trial. Prepare, My people, for your trial is about to begin."

Volume XI — Apr '98 to Jun '98

G7 Meeting (10 May '98) — plot for takeover in readiness for Antichrist.

P45 — "My people, this G7 meeting of your largest financial countries is about to trigger some future events. These evil men are continuing to plot the takeover of your world in readiness for the Antichrist to take charge. Wars or threats of wars will be used to scare people into giving their leaders emergency powers. This will be coupled with manipulated monetary instabilities to throw your markets into a panic. All of this will be planned as a means to have the evil ones gain control of your world."

Confession, sacramentals and physical needs to leave

"They know by certain means that their time is running out. Be prepared My faithful for some significant events to happen soon. Remember to be prepared in your soul by confession and physically with your sacramentals and physical needs to leave when events show you it is time.... Have no fear, but pray for courage and My protection. Follow only Me and never give in to belief in anyone else."

Volume XIII — Oct to Dec '98

The year of 666 — the sign of the Antichrist (666 x 3 = 1998)

P46 — "My people, I am showing you the sign of the man who will be the Antichrist. That sign is the number 666. You are in the year of 666 taken three times to give 1998. You have seen the Antichrist's sign of coming in the Hale-Bopp comet, as I have shown you. Prepare, My people, for the coming of the most *evil* man you have yet to see. He will have demonic powers and will try to have *everyone* worship him. Those who refuse to give him honour will be killed."

New money system and world government

"A new money system and a world government will be implemented to give power over all the food and jobs of the world. The age of the tribulation will see many demons unleashed from hell onto the Earth."

Volume XIII — Oct to Dec '98

Continuing disasters

P82 — "My people, your disasters will continue into the winter months, as many will lose their homes or have power outages making it hard to heat them. You will see these disasters affecting your food supplies, and scarcities will abound. Your economic problems will worsen all over the world, as your recessions will turn into a world depression. Any wars that occur will only worsen your difficulties. Pray now for My blessings and graces to be restored. But this will not happen until you return to your knees in prayer and stop the killing of My innocents in abortion. You will suffer a brief trial, so endure this in faith and I will bring you into My Era of Peace."

6. The Need to go into Hiding During the Tribulation

Volume I — Jul '93 to Jun '94

Jesus will instruct us where to go

P197 — "In the future times you may be forced to move to a safe haven away from your persecutors. Travel will be restricted for your own safety. I will instruct you in the future where you are to go. Have hope and trust in me that I will protect you and lead you to safety during this evil trial. It is your responsibility to remain faithful and concentrate on My Mother's triumph over Satan. Pray and keep My faithful close to My heart."

Volume II — Jul '94 to Jun '95

Pray to Jesus for help and to find a safe haven — be faithful

P39 — "The tribulation time will be your opportunity to witness to the strength of the love in Me. If you ask My help, I will lead you to a safe haven, so you will be protected from the onslaught of the demons. I will provide for you at that time much as I provided for My people during the Exodus. For I am a loving and caring God who will not let His faithful be orphaned. Just pray to Me and I will be at your side through all your troubles. Trust in Me and you will see My day of glory."

P64 — "My children, seek your protection underground both for protection from the evil men and the plagues I will send to the earth to torment man. I will direct you at the proper time where to be and what to do. Do not fear, My faithful, for I have promised to take care of you. This coming trial will be hard on all those who live through it. But My faithful remnant must stay true to My commands and give Me love and adoration."

P93 — "You will be seeking out to live in the fields and woods away from the evil authorities. You may think it not possible to survive without help, but with Me all things are possible. Also look for water and a hill to dig out a home in the ground. You must survive off the land but, if you cannot, I will provide for you. You may suffer for a short time, but once I take back control over evil, you will marvel in My plans of glory."

Do not worry about what to eat or where to stay. Jesus will provide

P100 — "My people, many will be in need of shelter with little time to provide for one. I have told you not to worry about what you are to eat or where you are to stay; I will provide for you. You will see miracles I will perform for you. I will make caves for you if you cannot make one or find one. The same with food. I will provide manna when none is available. I will be guiding your way much like God the Father helped the Israelites in the Exodus. Be confident in Me and pray for My help and you will receive it."

P107 — "Just as I gave up everything and roamed from place to place, you also will be nomads and have little possessions. In order to be free you will have to keep moving away from your persecutors. I will strip you of your possessions so you will have to place your trust in Me wholly for your survival, but you will see living your life to follow Me, even though you want stability, will be much less tedious. By giving your trust in faith to Me, I can feed you better both physically and spiritually. Follow Me wherever I take you."

Do not fear — take some basic necessities. Remain faithful to Jesus and He will lead us

P123 — "...I am telling you not to fear what will happen for I will be leading you. Do not fear either for others, for I will direct them as well. You may have to split into smaller groups to avoid detection. Where you go you will not be able to take your cars very far, since they are traceable to your whereabouts. Take some basic necessities, but do not worry. **I will provide for what you need.** The main concern is your care to remain faithful to Me to save your soul. In the end this is all that matters. To survive this time or not is not important…"

Be ready to go after the Warning. Take a shovel

P135 — "My people, I will always be watching over you even during the tribulation. Once the warning comes, be forewarned to make ready your preparations for hiding from the Antichrist and his agents. One of your necessities will be a shovel for areas where you dig out a house or tunnel. You must be below ground to avoid detection from helicopters and satellites who will be looking for My faithful. This also will serve as good protection from bombs or other chastisements."

We must put our trust in Jesus — don't worry where to go

P191 — "As the evil days close in on you, you will be sought out for torture or martyrdom. Do not worry what you are to say or where you are to go for I will provide for you. You will be asked to give up your possessions and the things of this world so you can serve Me only. This will be a time when you will need to put your full trust in Me and My word. It will be a time as in the Exodus when the Lord provided food, shelter and the direction for travel. Pray now to build up your spiritual courage, but live in hope for the day you will see My glory."

Take into hiding spiritual weapons and a few earthly helps

P304 — "My people, during the tribulation you will have to be resourceful to use what little you will have. Remember to take into hiding your spiritual weapons and a few earthly helps I have mentioned. Your trial may seem harsh but look what I had to go through for you. At that time it will be easy to distinguish the faithful from those in league with the evil one. By your love and sign on the forehead, you will recognise whom you can trust."

Volume III — Jul '95 to Jun '96

Do not worry about what to bring — Jesus will provide. Pray for help

P88 — "To survive, you must seek the countryside to live off the land, and what I will provide for you. Do not worry what you are to bring, since I will make up the difference of what you need. It is sufficient, My children, not to take the mark of the beast and put your trust wholly in My help. Pray for the help I will send My faithful through their angels. You will be led to safety away from the evil men. Be willing to give up everything you have, and you will save your soul, for no one can be written in the Book of Life, unless he comes to Me and denies his very self and the things of this world. Be attentive to your prayer life, and protect yourself spiritually from the coming evil trial."

Pray to our guardian angel to direct us. Electronic search instruments will be confused. Tracker dogs will not find us.

P104 — "When you go into hiding, My people, pray to your guardian angel to direct you. They will then lead you to safe places in such a way that no evil men will find you. Even if they should try to find you with their electronic devices, I will confuse their instruments. If they should send out tracking dogs for you, I will misdirect their attention and their sense of smell. I will go to great lengths to protect those who pray for My help. Seek Me at all times, and you will find My love and peace. All this I keep telling you so you will not lose heart, but see the power of having full faith and trust in Me. Pray for discernment in your problems, and I will help you in any of your concerns."

Reasons to be in hiding. A testing time. Pray and trust in Jesus

P119 — **The vision:** *Later I saw people walking slowly down a road in two columns, one on either side. They were not carrying any bags. Jesus said:* "My people, you are seeing the day when My faithful will be led out of the cities for torture and martyrdom. This is why I have given you many warnings and signs, to know when to go into hiding. Many will suffer in My name, but those who are wise, will find their way to safety beforehand. Look to the sign of apostasy, control of communications, weather disturbances and others described in Scripture. You will be tested, but My love and protection goes out to all to alleviate your concerns. Pray, My children, and I will come to your aid if you just have trust in My word."

All movements will be watched. Pray for protection

P125 — "My people, I am giving you a further warning during the tribulation. During this time there will be agents or spies looking for information on people. They will watch your every movement to know if you are a threat to their power. The evil people will see those that are religious as a threat, and so will either kill them or hold them in detention centres. If they cannot find you, they will send people to try and track your whereabouts. This is where I have told you in prayer that I will protect you from detection... Many evil things will occur, but with trust in My love, you will save your soul and be glorified with Me."

The permanent signs in the sky to mark safe havens. Pray much to be faithful

P127   **The vision:** *I could see miraculous lights in the sky during the tribulation. Jesus said:* "These lights will be the permanent signs of My presence for all, that they may keep their faith strong. These signs will be as beacons for you, so you can find safe havens from the evil ones. They will mark the places where My mother has appeared. These holy grounds and the hiding places you can find with My angels, will be your refuges where to find My help. Pray much in this evil age, that you will be faithful and always seek My help."

Powers of Antichrist. Strange lights from the heavens. Powers of suggestion

P140 — "My people, I give you a warning of what you are to expect at the coming of the evil one. You will see the Antichrist possess strange, unnatural powers, that will strike fear in some to believe in him. He will show strange lights from the heavens, and have great powers of suggestion almost as hypnotic powers. My angels will defend you, if you pray for their help, but you must avoid the evil one's powers by hiding, so he will have little influence on you. Those who are taken in by him will want to make him as a god to worship. These times will be difficult, but I will give you the strength to endure it. If you stay close to Me in prayer, with your blessed objects as I have directed, you will understand his reign is to be avoided. Then in a twinkling of an eye, I will crush him through My mother, and his reign will be no more."

Difficulty of travel — scanning for the Mark of the beast. Be in hiding

P154 — "My people, during the tribulation, you will find it difficult to travel in your car on the highways. You will find gates along the way, where the evil one's agents will be scanning people for the mark of the beast. When no identification number is found, they will at first send you to detention centres. If you are considered a threat to teach others of God, or your will cannot be moulded to the Antichrist, then they may martyr such people as an example. This is why, to avoid these agents, you must hide in caves or wooded areas with cover from detection. This will be a deep test of your physical and spiritual stamina, but you will not be alone. My angels and I will go with you, to support your efforts in living My message, even at the cost of being exiled.

"You will lose your former life for My sake, but you will find eternal peace at the judgement. When you witness to My word, I will not forget your allegiance to My will. Those who love Me, even if it may mean death, are the faithful remnants, that will carry on My Church until the judgement."

Great faith needed to save our souls. A time of purification

P222 — **The vision:** *"Later, I could see as if on an altar that there was a bright white cross that hung by itself without support. Below the cross there were many demons on either side."* Jesus said: "My people, I am showing you a picture of the time of the tribulation. **You will see My permanent sign of hope in the skies, that the demons will not be able to hide.** My faithful will be able to look upon it in their trial as Moses held up the dead seraph serpent on a pole. You will need a great faith supported through My grace and your prayer to save your souls at this time. Those who are lukewarm and without lasting roots in the faith will be swept away as straw in the wind of evil demons. This will be the world's purification when the demons will claim their own. They will torture and have their pleasure with these condemned souls."

Jesus' help — an urge to hide for our own safety. Pray much for conversion of souls

P292 — "My people, during the tribulation I will even give you an urge for your own safety, to go into the hills to hide. You will see how I will provide shelter for you, away from the evil spirits and the Antichrist's agents. I will blind their eyes to your whereabouts, but, for My faithful, I will almost lead them by the hand, through their angels, where you each are to go. Fear not where I will take you, for I will care for all of your needs…. Pray much for the conversion of souls, who will be part of My glory. These souls are hanging in the balance of the power of good and evil. Come to Me now, or you may be doomed to follow Satan into hell."

Hibernation during the tribulation

P318 — "My children, during the trial, I will help you to induce this phenomena so you can hibernate for long times without food. This will help you, since you cannot buy food then, and it will protect you from the evil ones, who are seeking you. Pray to Me for help and I will show you this protection. Do not be concerned about the details of how I will protect you, but have trust and faith. You are precious in My eyes and I will see to your needs. My children, pray for discernment and I will always lead you to safety."

Be prepared to leave everything and follow our angels

P328 — "My people, why do you have trouble believing that you must flee into the wilderness? You want to believe, but still you are attached to your possessions and you fear the unknown. Have no fear, My friends, for this will be a joyous time of faith in My protection. You must be as My apostles when I asked them to follow Me. You must be willing to drop everything at My word, and follow your angels as I lead you. I tell you, there will be some trials, but you will see this as a preparation in faith to lead your new lives on a renewed earth.... When you begin to understand My way of perfection, you will ask yourself: 'How could I have been so blind?' It is difficult to understand My perfection, since it is contrary to your current nature."

Volume IV — Jul '96 to Sep '96

Scorn of these messages. Follow Jesus

P28 — "My people, many times I have advised you to seek out caves for protection from the evil men, during the tribulation. Some have scorned this message from their pride and their fear. You know how much I love you and that I would not mislead you. Follow Me wherever I lead you, and you will never go wrong."

Volume VII — Apr '97 to Jun '97

Three signs of when to go into hiding

P41 — "Look to the signs of [1] the warning, [2] My Pope's exile and [3] this mark of the beast to know when to go into hiding. When you see these events, do not hesitate to go or you may risk being captured and attempts will be made to force you to worship the Antichrist. Fear not, for I will be with you."

Volume VIII — Jul '97 to Sep '97

They who hesitate to go may risk capture in detention centres

P39 — "...Be ready, My children, to flee when My Pope John Paul II leaves Rome and when evil people will be placing the mark of the beast on people. Those that hesitate to leave at these signs may risk capture in the detention centres. Have trust in Me and I will have your angels protect you. Do not fear, but have faith in My word."

Leave your possessions — Take into hiding only what you can carry

P57 — "My people ... You are to go into hiding with what you can carry. Be prepared most for your spiritual attacks with many sacramentals. Take your rosaries, crucifixes, holy water, Bibles, and blessed candles. Be prepared to leave your houses and cars behind. The more you trust in Me, I will provide for your physical and spiritual needs. It is this trust in My protection that will guard you."

7. The Plagues —
of locusts, scorpions and snakes

Revelation 9: 3-11

"Then from the smoke came locusts on the earth, and they were given authority like the authority of scorpions of the earth. They were told not to damage the grass of the earth or any green growth or any tree, but only those people who do not have the seal of God on their foreheads. They were allowed to torture them for five months, but not to kill them, and their torture was like the torture of a scorpion when it stings someone. And in those days people will seek death but will not find it; they will long to die, but death will flee from them."

Volume II — Jul '94 to Jun '95

Pestilence and plagues of locusts, scorpions

P75 — "My people, during the tribulation you will see many give praise and honour to the Antichrist. They will treat him as a god because of his miraculous powers. They will make sacrifices to him even, possibly, human sacrifices as they do even now in hidden places. I will send a curse upon these demented souls for blaspheming against Me. There will be many pestilences and plagues of locusts and scorpions which will be sent to bite and sting those accursed for their evil deeds. They will know that I am the Lord and I shall not have any strange gods before Me. Prepare, My people, for this evil time. You must muster all of your spiritual strength to endure it. I will shorten the time of this evil scourge lest even the elect would be lost. Believe in Me and I will save you through it all."

Volume IV — Jul to Sep '96

P38 — **The vision:** *"Later, I saw on the earth some huge flying locusts with stingers like scorpions. They were sent as one of the plagues that will torment all those who have turned against God. The locusts will sting these people short of death for a long time."*

Jesus said: "My people, you are seeing My justice carried out on those who have rejected Me and refused to obey My commands. I wish to show those souls, which have not been converted, what they will face in this tribulation. I ask all mankind to come to Me out of love, since I have made you and redeemed you with My Blood. You can also come to Me out of fear of My wrath and justice as well, but please come before it is too late.

"For those who will not give themselves over to Me, you will face a dreadful torture such that you will wish you had never been born. After these plagues, the unfaithful will suffer the purification by fire. This will be a taste of hell on earth for a short time. Then I will cast the evil spirits and these lost souls into the eternal fires of hell.

"You will see after time stops, that you will be in the eternal now. Those sent to hell will never escape, and they will have eternal torment from the flames and from the anger of the demons who hate man. So, My friends, you should realise what you are choosing, when you make life's decisions.

"Will you choose the delight of the body in this world, which will send you to eternal punishment with no peace, or will you choose to love Me or come out of fear, and you will see My paradise of love in My oneness and eternal peace and rest for your souls? The choice is yours, but remember the consequences of your decision, and do not be deceived by the evil one or the pleasures of the body."

Volume III — Jul '95 to Jun '96

Plagues of snakes

P195 — "My people, you are seeing in this vision another of the plagues which will be a part of the tribulation. This visitation of snakes will be in response to those who disbelieve in Me, much like those sent against the Israelites for rumbling against Me. As in that day, those who return to Me in this coming trial, will not have to fear their bites. But woe to those who still do not believe, for they will be in agony. Some will die as a result.

"All of these events will be a part of My plan for purifying the earth. Rejoice, My people, for Satan's reign is not much longer, then you will witness My glory and full reign of peace and love."

8. Electronic Communications —
TV, Radio, Computers, Internet
and Motor Vehicles

Volume I — Jul '93 to Jun '94

TV sets must be off when Antichrist comes. He will control minds through them

P22 — "The TV is being used by the demons to subvert the people. After the Antichrist comes to power, turn off your TV sets for he will control the people's minds even more powerfully through the viewing of him."

Hypnotism, demonic powers, electrical devices

P29 — "The Antichrist will have eyes which you should avoid. He will be able to hypnotise your thoughts and gain control of your mind. He will have demonic powers and you should hide from him. He and the men he will influence will seek out the faithful and try not only to kill the body but to steal the soul from God if they are not protected."

P186 — "Be watchful of all electrical devices which can be used to eavesdrop on you in your home. The government will be seeking information on you in their religious persecution. Beware of the abuse of even your cable TV in the future."

Volume II — Jul '94 to Jun '95

Manipulation of TV images. Virtual reality over TV

P38 — "They will be able to manipulate images on the TV to make those who watch believe anything they want you to. At this time, get rid of your cable and TV or you will come under their control."

P45 — "The Antichrist will exploit the use of virtual reality over the TV using it for mind control with earthly 'high' feelings. As I have told you, avoid this on your TV and probably get rid of them at that time for they will only be serving evil purposes."

P58 — "My people have slowly been led to a heightened sense of awareness in order to be impressed with TV programming and movies. These directors have increased the violence, sex and have changed lifestyles by their suggestions in these films. This evil has become so accepted that men have lost their awareness of what is sinful. It would be well for you not to watch TV or these movies. I am most displeased with it all."

Avoid use of Internet. Immorality of TV comedy

P109 — "Avoid the use of the Internet and all other forms of the future information highway. These will be the tools of the Antichrist and his agents to control your money and information on everyone."

P237 — "Do not be lulled to sleep spiritually in listening to your TV programs. Many such programs teach a wrong morality by comedy. While they are seemingly amusing, they are subtly destroying the morality of your country. You would better use your time in prayer than to weaken your faith."

P265 — "You wonder why crime and killing is so rampant in your streets, but I tell you look how you are training your children. Today, your TV programming glorifies sex, killing and horror stories. Do you think this has an influence on children as well as adults? The movie makers are most to blame. But it is the people who pay for this abuse and accept it, that makes it sell.

Increasing thresholds of wickedness

"With every passing day your society accepts a higher threshold of acceptance of this wickedness. Do you think this will go unanswered? Now you must fight against this abomination in your media. Protest to the sponsors and better yet, turn it off and pray for these people. They have been so ingrained with this filth that they no longer see anything wrong. Is it any wonder they do not come to confession when they do not know what sin is? Pray much, My people, for My justice will be coming against this evil generation."

Volume III — Jul '95 to Jun '96

Concern about use of Internet — a tool of the evil one. Subliminal messages. Avoid its use

P197 — "My son, several people have asked you why be concerned about using the Internet. Your media people have been encouraging many to hook up to this for the information highway. This is, and will become, a tool of the evil one when he comes to power. Curiosity will lead many to look for games and new experiences, especially virtual reality games. These will be quickly abused using subliminal messages to have people rely on this as a habit. Soon by the Antichrist's evil powers, he will trick many into sensual and other sins while they do not realize it.

"This is why I am telling you to avoid both the Internet and any communications the evil one can use to control you. At the tribulation, get rid of those electrical devices, which will let the evil spirits have influence over you through mind control. These evil spirits will overpower you if you do not avoid them and ask for My help. Pray to Me always and I will protect you from them. Have faith and trust in My word — it is all you will have."

Don't use Internet for personal messages

P293 — "My people, beware of the potential abuses of all your technical advances, especially the Internet. What seems a help now is becoming more global in its reach, as it is well positioned to be used by the Antichrist. This is why I have warned you to avoid using the Internet for personal messages. All of those messages can be recorded and used to harass you at a future time. Be forewarned of these problems and rely on My help to lead you."

Volume IV — Jul '96 to Sep '96

Dispense with all electronic communications at time of the tribulation

P6 — "My people, I have told you at the time of the tribulation to rid yourself of all electronic communications. This is how the

Antichrist will hold people in a trance, through hypnotic spells and subliminal messages. Be not afraid of the evil one, but ask for My help at all times and I will provide for your needs."

Volume VI — Jan '97 to Mar '97

Car number plates — special tracking devices

P50 — "My people, your car plates will have special electrical devices, so you can be tracked. Only those with the mark of the beast will be able to acquire them. That is another reason why your travel will be soon limited. Know that during the time of the Antichrist, you will be sought out for capture. I will be protecting you in safe places away from these evil men."

Volume VII — Apr '97 to Jun '97

Low earth orbit satellites — ability to track and immobilise new cars

P20 — "My people, I am showing in this vision how the authorities are sending more satellites into low orbit for their new communications network. By this means they will be able to track the location of all new cars. At will they also will be able to transmit frequencies to immobilise the chips running your car.

"These will be the same satellites used to monitor all the people with the chip in their smart cards or in the hand or forehead. Be aware not to take your car to your final destination of hiding since they will monitor your location. Also, do not take these smart cards or the chip in your body. All these things are a means of the Antichrist to control you. Refuse the mark of the beast or you will surely be lost. Do not worship anyone else but Me."

Detection devices in cars

P39 — "My people, while new cars serve their purpose, they are becoming a means for a new agenda by the one world people. More and more sophisticated devices are being placed in your car for detection devices. As you see this car [in the vision] abandoned in the fields, you know it can not be used to get you to your final hiding destination. Satellites will be tracking your car's whereabouts, so be forewarned. Have faith, My people and I will lead you to safety away from these evil men. I will protect you in ways unknown and I will frustrate man and his electrical devices."

Volume VIII — Jul '97 to Sep '97

Monitoring of public access lines. Loss of privacy and security

P27 — "My dear people, how quickly you have come to embrace all of your new found technological communications. Many of your advances seem to give outward advantages, but beware of the potential abuses of these new ways. Many of these public access lines will be monitored to control all of your calls and transactions. All of these electronic connections will no longer be protected. So, do not trust in man, but rather trust in God to lead you. When the evil one assumes power, all of these new advances will be used against you. Think soon that you will have to disconnect yourself with all of these electrical transmissions, since the Antichrist would control your mind. Plan now for your retreat into the wilderness for protection. Seek My help to guide you."

Computers and TV — built in means for two-way communication, even when turned off

P32 — "My people ... Many of your new TVs and computers have means for two-way communication. *Some have ways to view and listen to you even when it is turned off....* A time is coming, right before the Antichrist's coming, when you will have to get rid of all of your electrical devices. The Antichrist, by his powers of suggestion, will use your TVs to get you to worship him.... Seek My help in all of this tribulation, for without Me, you will be lost. Trust Me that My power will rule at all times. I will protect all of My faithful, but you will still have to suffer from persecution."

Transponders in newer cars for tracking

P39 — "...many of your newer cars have transponders in them so the evil people may be able to track where you are."

Volume IX — Oct '97 to Dec '97

The Antichrist's announcement of his coming declaration

P61 — "My people, I wish to warn you about the coming of the Antichrist and his declaration time. At the time of his first announcement about his coming in declaration, have all of your cables out of your house and do not watch your television any longer — disconnect them. As it comes closer to the day of his declaration, do away with your telephone lines, your computers, faxes, copiers, radios, and anything electronic that can be influenced by demons, since they will use them to distract you. In addition to these, stop your paper and even your mail. All of these again will be controlled.

Three signs of when to go into hiding

Remember, when you see [1] My warning, [2] Pope John Paul II leaving Rome, and [3] the placement of the chips in the hand, you are to pack your sacramentals and your physical needs, ready to go into hiding. Do not have any credit cards, smart cards, nor anyone with a chip in their body, since you can be tracked by these devices.

"Pray much during this trial for My help and I will instruct your angels where to take you for spiritual safety. This is a time to follow My instructions for helping to save your soul and those of your loved ones and friends."

9. The Tribulation —
Comets, Earthquakes, Volcanoes,
Diseases and Weather Control

Volume I — Jul '93 to Jun '94

The Atlantic comet — three days darkness. Events to speed up dramatically

P21 — "A comet will strike to Atlantic ocean and it will send out huge tidal waves. The burning trail will send up huge clouds of smoke which will cloud the sun for three days. Prepare and have your life in order."

P46 — "Events will speed up dramatically as the demons take power. Because of My people's sin and lack of prayer, there will be many chastisements sent to your land. You will be tested by fire such that it will seem like a raging inferno. **Those houses where prayer is said constantly, I will protect from the flames** — but woe to those houses that do not pray. The fires now in the west will pale in comparison to what will be coming. Some of this can be mitigated by prayer but not all. Start as many prayer groups as possible to stem the tide of the coming evil for it will exact My justice. I love My people always and am waiting for your love, but the lukewarm I detest."

Threats of World War III. Spiritual chaos reflected in the weather

P81 — "World War III hangs in the balance as a punishment for men's sins. The clouds of war and hatred are getting darker. Men are not praying enough for peace — on the contrary, they increase their greed for power and prestige. Until men humble themselves and pray to Me to restore order, wars will continue and get even worse. Without Me you can do nothing to stop these events. So send many prayers up for peace and harmony or you will reap the whirlwind of war."

P100 — "Record cold, heat, rainfall and snow will befall you. The weather is a reflection of the spiritual chaos in the lives of many. This is a worsening of the testing time which is coming upon you…. For My faithful who read these signs, know that I will forever protect those who do My will. Earthly things will be taken but I will give you the grace to endure these times. Keep faithful to My ways and I will reward you."

Shortening of Antichrist's reign. Pray constantly. Demons loosed from hell

P196 — "You are seeing [in the vision] the vehicle of My judgement of the earth. You will experience a cataclysmic event which will shorten the reign of Antichrist and his persecution of My faithful. Even though the earth will shudder and great events will be terrifying the inhabitants of earth, know that My ending of evil is near with this event…. You must pray constantly to withstand this time. Do not lose hope, I will be watching over you."

P225 — "During the tribulation, where I will purify the earth, the demons will be loosed from hell to roam the earth. They will be allowed to claim as their own those who have rejected Me and failed to repent of their sins. At the same time I will protect My faithful in their safe havens from the demons.... Some of the safe havens will be the holy ground where apparitions have occurred. Many angels from heaven and your guardian angels will be around also to protect you."

Volume II — Jul '94 to Jun '95

Comet of Jesus' judgement — now on track. Evil in the world

P20 — "My people, ... I have now already put on track a comet of My judgement which will strike the earth. No matter what your scientists will do, My justice will come with swift fury, for My people have allowed evil to choke their lives with too much care for worldly things. You are made to My image to adore Me, but you do not want to accept Me as My chosen people rejected Me also. Those faithful who know and love Me will be protected from My purification, but woe to those who blaspheme Me and utter all abominations, for they will taste of My wrath instead of My dinner."

P35 — "Rockets sent up by man to destroy the comet will be deflected by the angels."

Chastisement — Closeness of time of the comet. Resulting fumes. Difficulty breathing

P73 — "I am showing you again My chastisement not to frighten you but to tell you it is close for the comet to come. You will be joyous once it arrives, as it will bring My Coming that much sooner. I have shown you the path of fire and the resulting fumes which will choke some as the sun's light will cease for a time. Be in a spot protected from the air so you do not have to breath these fumes. Much of the oxygen will be consumed and breathing will be difficult, but once this trial has passed, you will be resplendent in My glory, for no one can imagine how beautiful life will be for My faithful. On the other hand, those not loyal will meet a bitter fate."

Change in earth orbit. A great coldness. Prepare with warm clothes

P147 — "You are seeing a picture of the final chastisement when a cataclysm will strike the planet. In the process the earth will be veiled in darkness and a collision will cause it to go out of its normal orbit for a time. You will see a great coldness come over the earth, so prepare with warm clothes and blankets. Fear not, My children, the earth must be purified before I renew it. Pray and I will watch over you."

Volume IV — Jul '96 to Sep '96

Volcanic eruptions. Distortion of earth's crust. Change in magnetic poles

P11 — "My son, you are seeing a massive volcanic eruption in this vision where dark smoke was evolving. It is true that you will continue to see volcanic eruptions increase, but this one will occur as the comet strikes the earth. There will be a tremendous distortion of the earth's crust which will give rise to many such volcanoes. It will be a combination of these eruptions and the comet's own debris that will give rise to the three days of darkness. Other repercussions will be a changing of the magnetic poles from their present position, and also a brief change in the earth's orbit away from the sun. The gravity of the sun will correct this change in orbit, but for a while the earth will be colder.

"It is during these three days of darkness that a cave or underground dwelling will afford you best protection from the cold and the sulphur in the air depleting the oxygen for a short duration. Pray, My people, and listen to My instructions, and I will direct you where to go and how I will feed you with My Heavenly Bread."

Increasing frequency and intensity of earthquakes. Work to save souls

P51 — "My people, you are again seeing another sign of the end times in this vision. Earthquakes have been occurring with a higher frequency. They, also, will be increasing in intensity. There will be some severe earthquakes possibly in the Pacific Ocean which may cause some flooding in some areas.... Again, I tell you that many of these chastisements will fall on areas of greater sin. Hear

My plea for prayers, so you can pray for peace and the conversion of sinners. Never lose sight of working to save souls around you, especially in your own families."

Contagious diseases. Blood red moon a sign of the tribulation

P70 — "My people, during these days of purification, you will see many strange diseases afflict the people. Many will be stricken, and contagious diseases will spread among you like wildfire. See these tests again as trials in your tribulation. If you look on My cross, or pray to your angels, these diseases will be cured."

P70 — "My people, look to the sky for the signs of My visitation. When you see the moon turn blood red, it will be a sign to you of the tribulation among you. Evil men will spread their hate among you, but My love will guard you against them. Have faith in My help even amidst the darkness of evil. This, also, will be a sign of the wars that will be all over the land."

Tesla weather machines. Weather and food manipulation

P79 — "My people, I have warned you that some of your food problems may be contrived. You may have thought that food supplies may be controlled to create shortages. In your vision you are seeing [how] an even more devious means of controlling food could be done by controlling your weather. These machines [the Tesla weather machines] can influence your weather through various wave patterns put out by huge electromagnets.

"You have men in various places who are planning to use these devices in destabilising your weather patterns. Evil has reached new levels of controlling people by their electrical devices. Pray, My people for deliverance from such evil men. Even despite all of their devious plans, I will use ways to thwart them from reaching their goal of world control. I will baffle their devices, so many will not even work."

Volume V — Oct '96 to Dec '96

Speed up of events — few will understand. Let Jesus rule our lives

P61 — "...If you were noticing, you would see how rapidly events are continuing, even now. Remember, I warned you that events would speed up in the end times. If you are a student of your own times, you would recognise these happenings. You are indeed waiting for events that you would recognise as more serious, and as defined in My Scriptures. Have patience, for these times are arriving, but few of My faithful will understand these events. This is in keeping with My Scriptures, that the clever will be confused and the simple will have great understanding. It is not the proud or the rich who will inherit the earth but My humble faithful who obediently follow My every wish. If you seek salvation in heaven, you must come to Me and give your will over to Me. When you let Me rule your life, then the beauty of My understanding will be made clear to you...."

P62 — "My friends, you are in the thick of battle for souls with the evil one. You have many signs of immorality and killings all around you. Were you to deny this era as evil, like Sodom and Gomorrah, you would be a liar. Again, you are without doubt in the end times, since never before in your history, have you seen such events. You have seen an unparalleled increase in knowledge of science, more earthquakes than historical records show, many changes in your weather, famines in Africa and elsewhere, comets hitting Jupiter and many other omens in the sky.

Jesus' Second Coming. Return to confession

"Again, if you think these are not the end times, you are sadly mistaken. My Second Coming is not far off, since my mother has warned you in many sites of apparition. Be forewarned about these signs, but most of all return to Me in confession, where I will forgive your sins, so you can be spiritually prepared to do battle for your soul. Those who do not prepare will be swept away in ruin like the man who built his house on sand."

Volume VII — Apr '97 to Jun '97

The comet - beginning of three days of darkness. Result of comet in Atlantic Ocean

P9 — **The vision**: *"I had several views of a huge wave of water which was revealed to me as coming from the great chastisement of the earth. Jesus said:* "My people, what you are seeing will be a part of the great miracle of My final triumph over Satan and his followers. Because this wave of destruction will fall against your eastern seaboard, it would be wise to have a dwelling high and further inland. This will begin the days of darkness as a result of the comet striking the earth in the Atlantic Ocean. The earth's judgement is coming with a great purification. Prepare now while you still have time."

The comet — announcement by astronomers. Many lives lost
P13 — "My people, prepare for the coming chastisement that will end evil on this planet.... Look to the skies and be attentive to the astronomers, when this comet will fall on you out of the sky. My justice is coming and it will soon be visible to your eyes. Many events will test your faith, but this will be the most serious and destructive. Many lives will be lost, but I will be at your side giving you My peace. Know that the earth must be cleansed of the evil that permeates it."

Volume VIII — Jul '97 to Sep '97

The comet — already on its way. Angels will deflect attempts to destroy
P45 — "My people, I am showing you the comet of the great chastisement. It is already directed towards Earth and it will not be changed from its orbit. It will not be long and you will hear of its discovery. At first it will be kept secret so as not to raise fear among the people. The information will be leaked out as the military will try to destroy it. I have shown you before that My angels will deflect any attempts to destroy it. Do not be fearful, My children, but be in preparation. Those in the caves would be most protected. This is the instrument that I will use to thwart Satan of his brief reign. Continue to prepare spiritually, for you know not the time I will call you home to Me."

Volcanoes, huge earthquakes — will reshape the dry land
P57 — "My people, you will see great changes made on the Earth's surface as huge earthquakes and volcanoes will reshape the dry land. There will be much death and suffering when these great

disturbances will occur. There will be nothing you can do because these things will take place swiftly with no warning. Be ever prepared spiritually, because you know not when you will be called home to judgement. So continue your frequent confessions so your souls are always ready to receive Me."

Violence in weather reflects society
P66 — "My people, these storms you can sense are near. Every day you are reading about violence with guns in the streets. There is continued violence still being done to the unborn, but it is kept secret. There are even signs of continued preparation for nuclear war. I have told you before that your weather will turn violent as you have become a violent people. So do not be surprised that the violence in your weather reflects your society. You need to be on your knees more in prayer or your society will consume itself in chaos."

California earthquake
P74 — "My people, you must be prepared for the events about to unfold. I have given you warning before about an earthquake that will be coming in California. This will be severe and its timing is near. Many people there will be shaken out of their complacency. There will be much destruction and many will lose heavily in their material possessions."

The end times. A quick succession of events. Trust in Jesus' protection
P75 — "My people, I have told you in these end times that you will see one event right after the other in quick succession. You are seeing volcanoes, earthquakes and other storms coming together. These again are signs of the end times, but the people are not looking to Scripture for this interpretation. Wake up, My people and see that your time of tribulation draws near. Even though these events will be closing in on you, have trust in My protection when this destruction meets a fever's pitch."

Diseases and pestilences. Vaccine resistant strains of germs. Much terror and chaos
P83 — "My people, beware of the coming diseases and pestilences that will be coming in the last days. You will see new vaccine resis-

tant strains of germs that will again cause huge epidemics of sickness. Even some diseases will be brought about through germ warfare. Your manipulation of the genes in medicines and plants will be another cause for concern. Those gifted with healing these diseases will be sought out.

"See, those who defy My love will have to suffer many plagues here as their punishment at the end of this age. As many will die from these outbreaks, there will be much chaos and terror for those who survive. Be faithful to Me in adoration and in your prayers, and I will protect you from these new germs. See that all these things will happen to confuse the proud and bring low those seeking fame."

Volume IX — Oct to Dec '97

The three days of Darkness. Only blessed candles. The Era of Peace

P35 — "My people, what I am showing you is the beginning of the three days of darkness. After the comet strikes, there will be a massive volcanic activity. You will see the fire of the volcanoes on the horizon. As much dust and ash will be released into the air, then the sun will be completely blotted out. It is at that time that you need to be inside and not looking out at the lost souls who will be burning in a living Hell on earth.

"Only blessed candles will give light at that time. Have faith that I will protect My faithful during this cataclysm. After the plagues of revelation are over, I will chain Satan, his demons and all the evil people in Hell. Then the renewal of the earth will take place, and I will bring My faithful back to a renewed earth as the Era of Peace will begin. Rejoice, My people, for those living at this time will enjoy paradise on earth as Adam experienced."

Volume X — Jan '98 to Mar '98

P79 — "My people, your diseases will begin to multiply and many will fall sick and die. Some of your outbreaks will be caused by man and some by nature. You will see a pestilence of disease grow across your nation and other nations. Many will die before cures will be found. There will be little defence from these sick-nesses, as they will die out as quickly as they came."

Drug resistant mutations of diseases. Mutations added to older diseases

P94 — "My people, you are seeing various diseases that are going to be increasing. Some diseases will increase because of the many changes in your weather and as a consequence from disas-ters. Some older diseases will come back stronger with more drug resistant mutations. Another source of disease will come from germ warfare instigated by the one world people who are creating panic in order to implement a world takeover. There are insidious people behind the scenes trying to reduce the population of the world for their own agenda. They are the same ones that are adding muta-tions to older diseases. Man will reap the consequences of this behaviour, as world pestilence will come over the land. You have abused the natural order of balance in nature and you will see dis-eases attack in epidemics."

Epidemics of air-borne diseases. Lack of medicines. Cures at caves and safe havens

P96 — "My people, you will see a day coming soon when air-borne diseases will travel quickly over many people. There will come such epidemics that there will not be enough medicine to stop this sickness. Some of these epidemics will be started by germ warfare. Isolation from the sick will be your only defence. As the time of the tribulation arrives, this will be another reason to go into hiding. At all the safe havens and caves, all your sickness will be miraculously cured. As the pestilence of famine and disease spreads over the land, these places of My protection will be sought by many of My faithful. Have faith and trust in My help and you will have everything provided for you."

Volume XII — Jul to Sep '98

Germ warfare. Healing of plagues and diseases

P70 — "My people, there will be attempts by your military to start spreading germ warfare in various parts of your country as 'experiments'. As the time of the tribulation draws near, these evil men will be spreading disease germs in rural areas where they suspect My faithful are hiding.

"You will be protected by My angels at all of My safe havens and the caves from any sickness. Look on the luminous crosses or drink the healing waters at the caves, and you will be healed of any plagues or diseases. You will be safe at these places from any weapons or detection equipment. Have trust in My help to protect your bodies and your souls from evil men and the demons. Pray for my help at all times, and your souls will be saved."

10. Armageddon

Revelation 16: 13-16

"I saw three unclean spirits like frogs come from the mouth of the dragon, from the mouth of the beast, and from the mouth of the false prophet. These were demonic spirits who performed signs. They went out to the kings of the whole world to assemble them for the battle on the great day of God the almighty... They then assembled the kings in the place that is named Armageddon in Hebrew."

"Then I saw the beast and the kings of the earth and their armies gathered to fight against the one riding the horse and against his army. The beast was caught and with it the false prophet who had performed in its sight the signs by which he had led astray those who had accepted the mark of the beast and those who had worshipped its image. The two were thrown alive into the fiery pool burning with sulphur. The rest were killed by the sword that came out of the mouth of the one riding the horse, and all the birds gorged themselves on their flesh."

Volume I — Jul '93 to Jun '94

Unrest in the Mid-East will culminate in the battle of Armageddon

P193 — **The vision:** ... *I saw a crucifix and it turned into a sphinx-like Egyptian and then into an Arab with the white headpiece.*

"Those who are students of history realise there will never be peace in the Mid-East since each claim it to be their own. There will continue to be unrest in that area of the world. It will all culminate in the battle of battles at Armageddon between the good forces and the evil forces. Just as the Antichrist and his legions seem poised to win, I will intervene and start his downfall. I have told you he will rise to power for a time, but it will not last long. The evil testing must be shortened to save My elect. This is a messages of hope in the end but a trial for a period of time. Continue to pray constantly and keep close to Me. Being a part of My will and My body is indeed My calling to you always."

Volume II — Jul '94 to Jun '95

All the people of the earth will be drawn into the conflict

P16 — **The vision:** ... *I saw a demonic-looking face which had eyes which sparkled with green rays emanating from them. This was a picture of the Antichrist. I then saw a very clear brilliant white cross signifying Jesus' victory over him. The demonic face became one of fright as I saw a deep pit and he was thrown into the abyss.* "You, My people, are almost at the time of the Antichrist as foretold in the Scriptures, for he will have an appointed time in history which I will allow. This will not be a time for the weak of faith. Once the evil one comes to power, many will be drawn to him because of his seeming miraculous powers. My faithful must seek My protection at this time in My Eucharist where it can be found, My Mother's rosary, and help from your guardian angels. This will truly be a test of your will to choose Me and trust in My word, for there will ensue a great battle of good and evil at Armageddon. **All the people of the earth will be drawn into this conflict between Antichrist and My warriors.** At that time, the Antichrist will be defeated and a great cataclysm will occur that will wipe out his forces."

P17 — "I will enter to claim the victory over him and he will be dashed with all who are evil in My sight into the fires prepared for Satan and his angels. At this time, I will renew the earth and there will be My Mother's triumph as she promised. This will be an era of peace free from corruption where all My faithful will live in love and adoration of Me. It will be as heaven on earth. Pray My people that you will be vigilant in prayer and you will see Me just as I have promised you."

Many angels will be in the battle led by St. Michael

P57 — "This Battle of Armageddon will be fought for control of the people. Many angels will be in the battle led by St. Michael. It will represent the turning point in Satan's reign and his power over the earth... Prepare always with prayer for you will need a great strength of character and My help to win the battle over evil."

Volume III — Jul '95 to Jun '96

Gas and oil shortages. Many things will be horse driven

P185 — "I am showing this vision, My people, so you can see the result of all your hate and greed. Man is heading for World War III by his lust for power and greed for money. If there is not enough prayer for peace, a nuclear disaster could be in your future. There will be a war, but its severity can be mitigated with your prayers. See to it, My people, that you desire My peace over that of Satan. I also am showing you in thought, that the war of Armageddon will be different, since gas and oil will be scarce at that time. Many things will be horse driven and will be ripe for control. I have told you that at that time My triumph will overcome Satan and his forces will be defeated. Then he will no longer take an active role in your lives, for My triumph will be total and usher in My Mother's triumph in an era of My peace and love."

Angels able to defend the faithful with the full force of their power

P255 — "My people, the battle between good and evil grows more intense. You will gradually see a clear-cut division between each of these spiritual forces. It will soon come to a point, when evil spirits are loosed, that I will also loose the ability of My own angels to defend My faithful with their full force, without restrictions as now. I will allow each soul freedom to choose Me or not, such that angels on either side will not be able to force your will. See this as a great opportunity to show your faith in My help, since this will be your only recourse during the trial. You will see events gradually lead up to the final Battle of Armageddon, as then My victory will be proclaimed over sin and Satan. This conquest will be as astounding as the glory of My Resurrection..."

Volume VII — Apr to Jun '97

Israel — the land of the Battle of Armageddon

P62 — "My people, keep your gaze fixed on the country of My people, Israel. It will be in this land that the final Battle of Armageddon will occur. When a spiritual war breaks out involving many nations, be attentive that your end times may be drawing close. This is the last battle among men before I come in triumph to cast Satan and the demons into hell. Rejoice when you see these events."

Volume VIII — Jul to Sep '97

Satan's time about to end. The Antichrist's declaration

P41 — "Know that the evil one will have his hand in bringing discord at this time. Satan's time is about to come to an end and he will be unleashing all his fury against man, shortly. Look to the seeds of this last Battle of Armageddon. The time of the Antichrist's declaration is not far off. You must come to Me in love to seek protection from all of these hateful factions. The power struggles between good and evil are about to clash."

The site of the Battle of Armageddon. The demons and the evil men will be chained in Hell

P91 — **The vision:** *"... I could see some very tall mountains on opposite side. Down the middle there was a great plain that had several large heart shapes."*

P91 — "My people, this vision is showing you the site of an awesome battle that will take place as the Antichrist seeks full reign of the world. The hearts on the battlefield indicate how My help and My angels will assist the good forces in defeating evil. Have trust, My people, that I will come to your aid and your protection will be assured. This final battle of good and evil at Armageddon will decide once and for all the almighty power that God has over all creatures. It is God's will that will be done, and the demons and evil men will be chained in Hell. There will be no dispute over who reigns over the world, for My triumph will rise over the heaped bodies of My enemies. My glory will shine forth over all the Earth, as it will once again be made over into the Kingdom that it was meant to be."

Volume XIII — Oct to Dec '98

Iraq — its use by the one world people. Muslims and communist nations to unite against the West

P77 — "My people, your armaments in the region around Iraq are like a tinderbox about to explode. From day one this area has been very delicate near all of the world's largest oilfields. It is for this reason that the one world people have been using Iraq as a means to bring acceptability to the New World Order. I told you before that these evil men will cause an excuse to bring war to this region once again. It will then be a matter of your prayers and the parties involved to reach a compromise, that will determine the extent of this war. Events are about to increase dramatically as Satan's time is running out. There will be one last attempt by the Antichrist for the one world people to take control of the world by force. The Muslim peoples and the communist nations will then unite against the western nations. This will culminate in a battle in Israel on the Plains of Armageddon.

"Did you doubt that this part of the Scriptures would be fulfilled? But in the end I will be victorious over all evil and the evil ones will be cast into Hell. Take courage, My children, for Satan may seem to be winning the battle, but I will win the war. Rejoice, My faithful, for My victory will assure your entry into My new Era of Peace. Follow My commands and My will, and you will live in My peace and love forever."

Volume XIV — Jan to Mar '99

The evil men and demons against the holy angels and faithful warriors

P37 — "My people, you have heard of the legion of demons I cast out of the possessed man in the Gospel. I am showing you in this vision how the many demons in hell will be unleashed onto the earth to test mankind's faith during the tribulation. I told you that the evil of the tribulation will be so severe, that you would not have to ask when is the tribulation?

"It will be because demons were released that you will need My help and that of your guardian angel in order to save your soul. Even though evil will have its short reign, do not be fearful, since I will always be available for your protection. It will be a combination of evil men and these demons that will direct the battle of Armageddon against My holy angels and My faithful warriors. My triumphant comet of chastisement will then fall on the Earth, confounding all the evil people with darkness. All the evil spirits and evil people refusing My love will be separated and chained in hell. I will then bring about My new heavens and new earth, as My Era of Peace will then reign over the Earth."

Satan will be defeated and he and his forces will be chained in Hell. Trust in Jesus' miraculous help

P91 — "My people, I am showing you this array of soldiers so you can see My angels assembling for the Battle of Armageddon. I will provide you My warriors to fight your battles against Satan and his demons. A time is coming when Satan will be defeated and all of his forces and himself will be chained in hell by My angels. The last chastisement will bring down a black curtain on all of the earth. All of the evil spirits and the evil people will be wiped from the face of the earth in My victorious triumph. Fear not the evil ones, when you have Me at your side fighting your battles. There will be a time of testing and uncertainty during the tribulation, but by remaining faithful to Me, you will have no worries. Trust in My miraculous help in those days and I will share My reward with you in heaven and on earth."

18 Jan 2000

The power of the angels. Listen to their prompting. The Battle of Armageddon and the Era of Peace.

"My people, I want to show you the joy of My heavenly court that will be guarding and guiding you through the time of tribulation. You will not be alone, so have no fear as the time for the Antichrist draws near. One of My angels has a lot more power through My grace than many demons. You each are assigned your own guardian angel to watch over your every action. Listen to their prompting to live good spiritual lives.

"Just as you receive temptations from the evil one, so My angels suggest ways to bring your soul closer to Me. Call on My angels and the saints when you need to be comforted or protected from any demonic encounters. My angels are always ready to help you in your spiritual battle for souls.

"**The battle of Armageddon** looms in the Middle East and the battle lines are being drawn. It will be My triumph over these evil ones that will begin My new Era of Peace. Trust in Me that I will have My angels separate out the evil tares from the wheat of My flock. These evil ones will be chained in hell, while My faithful will have their reward in heaven and on earth."

11. The Era of Peace

Revelation 21: 1- 4

> *"Then I saw a new heaven and a new earth; the first heaven and the first earth had passed away, and the sea was no more. And I saw the holy city, the new Jerusalem, coming down from heaven from God, prepared as a bride adorned for her husband. And I heard a loud voice from the throne saying, "See, the home of God is among mortals. He will dwell with them as their God; they will be his peoples, and God himself will be with them; he will wipe every tear from their eyes. Death will be no more; mourning and crying and pain will be no more, for the first things have passed away."*

Volume VIII — Jul to Sep '97

P96 — **"The promise of My Kingdom is upon you.** You should be rejoicing at the thought of the new Era of Peace that will be coming in the near future."

Volume I — Jul '93 to Jun '94

P15 — "An era of peace will come over the earth after it is purified by fire."

P108 — **The vision:** *"Later I saw a priest dressed in white at first and we were entering into a beautiful white ramp which was bright without a light source. It was then I could see a beautiful earth as we all could see it. It was restored to its former beauty. Even at night there was a glow from God that lit the night."*

"This is a view of what heaven and earth will be during the reign of peace which will be My Mother's triumph. You will see Me clearly and your joy will know no bounds. Peace will permeate you with My love. You will experience no sin or temptation. You will not worry about what to eat or wear for everything will be provided. You will be able to pray unimpeded by merely opening your mind to Me. Life will be glorious for you then as it was initially intended. This will be a beautiful time of fellowship as the whole community will be of one mind directed to My will. This will be a foretaste of heaven which will come at the end of time as you know it. Pray and offer sacrifices that you will be worthy enough to merit this gift of My love to My chosen."

It will come in John Leary's lifetime — but at a high price of endurance

P132 — "A new dawn is coming on an era of peace. This will be a supernatural experience.... It will be a time when the purified earth will be free of its present corruption. **It will be as I originally intended before the fall of Adam.** It will occur within your [John Leary's] lifetime. It will be a joy for those faithful to live during this time. But it will come at a high price of endurance. The earth must go through the pain of My persecution and suffering in order for those faithful to persevere. With prayer and allegiance to My will, you will win the prize of salvation for your souls."

It will come with Mary's triumph. Many will be tested to the limit

P151 — "There will be an era of peace ushered in at My Mother's triumph. But there will be a fierce battle of good and evil before that time. You must prepare as I have warned you before for this battle. Many of My faithful will be tested to the limit. You must rely on My help to endure it. But do not worry over that day for I will give you the strength to endure the demons' attempts to destroy you. Live for the hope to see My day in peace and that should be enough to sustain you. Stay close to Me in prayer and the sacraments."

After Mary's triumph it will be as for the Garden of Eden

P169 — "But after this short time there will be a new earth. My Mother will crush the head of Satan and the demons will be locked away in hell. **A peace and My Mother's triumph will reign for a millennium.** My faithful will then enjoy peace on earth as intended for the Garden of Eden. This will be a taste of your reward for suffering on earth and doing My will. Be faithful and endure this trial for your reward will be great."

A dramatic facelift of the earth. Restored to its former beauty. No evil

P194 — "Eye has not seen nor ear heard of the glory and peace I will bring to My people. After a brief tribulation, My elect who have been faithful in following the narrow road will celebrate with Me My Mother's triumph. **It is impossible for you to understand such a dramatic facelift of your earth but believe it is coming.** This era will resemble My Garden of Eden. The earth will be restored to its former beauty. All evil will be removed.

No anger, no sickness, no death, no killing

"There will be no anger, no death, no sickness, no killing — nothing but a sharing of My love with My people. You will have the opportunity to see Me again face to face and My glory will know no bounds. Pray that you live for this moment. It will indeed be a grace to experience this glory — but you must choose Me now over the world to graduate to My happiness for you. Pray and bring all you can into the hope of sharing My day."

Volume II — Jul '94 to Jun '95

P46 — **The vision:** *"...I saw what looked like a great ball of exploding energy, but as the vision continued there was no mush-*

room cloud. This seemed to be an ever expanding energy of Divine nature which seemed to spread over the whole earth as it was being renewed."

"This renewal of the earth will come after the tribulation and the devil and his people have been purified from the earth. I will restore the earth to its once pristine beauty at the time of Adam. It will be free from man's pollution and destruction of the animal species. **Everything will once again live in complete harmony.** You will see that this will be a time of hope for all to enjoy at My command. Just as the prophets enkindled the dead bones back to life, I will restore the earth and all My faithful will return who died in the tribulation."

Abundance of food. No need to work to eat

"Then there will be an era of peace, which will be like heaven on earth since I will communicate with man much as I did with Adam and Eve. **You will no longer fear death or sickness. Food will be abundant without having to work.** This will be My first reward to all those who remained faithful to Me during the trial. Knowing this message should heighten your faith and trust in My word that I will protect and watch over you always. All I ask is that you pray and keep Me in your thoughts at all times."

Volume III — Jul '95 to Jun '96

P276 — **The vision:** *"...I could see a huge plane or spaceship, leaving the earth behind on a journey into space."*

"My people, this vision is another witness of how I will protect you in the end times. **Right before I renew the earth, I will take My faithful up to a safe place.** When you see My love and care made manifest for you, you will understand why I tell you now to have no fear for where you are going. My protection, through My angels, will be constantly watching over you. As you are carried off, I will renew the earth to a paradise you cannot imagine."

A taste of Heaven before the final judgement

"This era of peace and love will be a taste of heaven before the final judgement. This, also, is My reward to all of those who remained faithful to Me in the tribulation. See this message as one of glorious hope in My promises to My people. Those who accept Me and follow My will will have a splendour of joy awaiting them in My era of peace. Live for this moment, when My justice will prevail and evil will have no more influence on you."

P314 — **The vision:** *"...Later I was walking in a magnificent garden which seemed endless. Everything was peaceful and glorious.*

"My son, you are experiencing how it will be during the era of peace. This will be your reward for being faithful during the tribulation, and it will show you how I intend life to be for all mankind. You will see Me walking in the garden, such that each of you will see Me everyday in My glory. During the day, you may call on Me in prayer at any time, even by your very thoughts. Some may ask what they will be doing during this time. You will be like the angels in awe of My power, My peace and the splendour of My creation."

Full knowledge and understanding

"Because you will have full knowledge to understand Me better and your renewed earth, many will be constantly kneeling in adoration and thanksgiving to Me. I am letting you fully sense this feeling of complete love and peace, so you can witness to My people what they have to look forward to after My victory. Keep your hope in My love always and never forget that what I have in store for you is beyond anything you could imagine. Give Me your trust now, and live only to please Me by following My will."

Volume IV — Jul to Sep '96

All on earth will be in harmony. Animals will not kill each other for food. Man will not need to eat

P67 — "I have told you how man will be in harmony with Me and himself. **You will be young again and perfectly formed, so you will not experience death or sickness.** Eating to survive will not be necessary, so that you will be a vegetarian if you choose to eat. All the animals around you will be perfected, and young as you with no death or sickness. Animals will not kill each other for food, since they also will not require food for survival. All on earth will be in harmony with My will, as it was before Adam's fall.

A beauty among nature beyond our wildest dreams. Every animal will be precious

You will see a beauty among nature that you cannot now fully appreciate. **Every animal, down to the last insect, will be precious to Me, and you shall not destroy any of them.** Instead, you will have full knowledge and understand why they must be as you are, existing free of any evil threats. When you live in My divine will, you will be experiencing the perfection that I desire of you on earth. See this life and the era of peace as a preparation for your entry into heaven, to enjoy My presence in the eternal now."

Volume V — Oct to Dec '96

The old will look younger. Children will mature in their thirties. All will be in perfect harmony

P6 — "This is an age where all men will experience the time before Adam's sin on a renewed earth. Older people will be strengthened to look younger, and the children will mature in their thirties. The animals and man will live in perfect harmony at that time. You will be able to call on Me and I will answer you at any time. You will be exposed to full knowledge of My universe. You will live to an old age and many will live to the end of this age. You will experience My love and peace, so you will be as heaven on earth. You will see in this age how I intended the world to be without the influence of evil."

No wars. Only the faithful will be brought back to life with glorified bodies

"When you are truly faced with the glory of My Creation, you will choose to please Me in every facet of your life. Time will continue, but there will be no wars, as you will love your neighbour as you love Me. Only My faithful will be brought back to life with glorified bodies. You will have time to adore Me and serve Me every day. You will be giving Me thanks continually that you been graced to be present in this age. This is a message of hope I am showing you, so that My faithful, who have been purified, will enjoy their reward in My splendour of My Kingdom."

Glorified bodies of those who have died. Those faithful through the tribulation will have rejuvenated bodies

P7 — "Those who have died and are resurrected will have glorified bodies and will live to the end of this era. Those who are faithful and live through the tribulation will have their reward also in My era of peace. These will have their bodies rejuvenated and will live long lives. It is only some of these people who may see death before the end of this era. Do not be concerned over the details of how My Will intends things. It is My keeping with Scripture and My promises that are more important."

Volume XI — Apr to Jun '98

The New Jerusalem. The temperature will be perfect. Full knowledge and understanding of life

P82 — "My people, I have told you that I will create a new Jerusalem that I will bring down to earth. It will be made of many rare stones and its walls will gleam with My light. Those that live in the Era of Peace will be spiritually fulfilled to see My peace and love on earth without any evil. You will all be witnesses of My splendour as you grow in perfection."

"My people, look with eager anticipation for when My faithful will live in My new Era of Peace. **You will have perfect temperatures at all times. Vegetation will be all about you and it will replenish itself.** You will enjoy the beauty of creation with a full knowledge and understanding of how life works. You will live long lives because you will have the advantage of My Garden of Eden with all its life giving elements."

Temples of light and places of worship — anytime day or night. No fear of animals

P82 — "My people, this is another scene of the Era of Peace, where you will experience temples of light and places to worship Me at any time day or night. You will have no fear of any war again. Even your fear of animals will be removed as you can caress any of them without any bites or any stings. The harmony of this world will so overwhelm you, to see how everything can be without the effect of evil."

Volume XIII — Jul to Sep '98

The age we live in will become the New Era of Peace. The new Jerusalem

P73 — "This week in My Church is judgement week when the readings are very explicit about My coming in glory. It is true that the age you are in will be changed into My new Era of Peace, but it will not be the end of time yet. At My triumph over Satan and the Antichrist, all evil spirits and evil humans in their souls will be cast into hell. My new Jerusalem will bring My faithful down to a re-created earth and there will be a reign of peace in a paradise. This will be a preparation of My faithful to live in My divine will and then, at the end of My Era of Peace, they will come to heaven. Those that follow My will should rejoice to be saved and enjoy eternity with Me in heaven."

Part II

Supplementary Messages

Confession 96

The Divine Will 104

The Priesthood, the Mass, the Real Presence,
    Exposition, Morals 108

The Mass — Underground Masses 113

Abortion 120

Children 126

Suffering in our lives 134

Understanding the Great Tribulation and the Era of Peace

Index to Some of the Messages to John Leary — Part II

Confession

Page   **Subject**

96   Confession at least once a month. Avoid the sin of sacrilege. **Souls in hell for sins of the flesh.** Only those who ask forgiveness can be forgiven. Preparation for the warning by confession. Many souls go to hell. Go to the priest in confession. Contrition necessary.

97   Be sorry for your sins and Jesus will forgive them. Freedom from sins ready for Jesus' protection. **What is sin?** All sins of the flesh are mortal sins.

98   **Make a monthly habit of confession.** Seek forgiveness of sin. Confession — the only hope to right ourselves before the warning.

99   All who wish to convert will be accepted. Jesus will always forgive the repentant sinner. Be not afraid. Sinners do not wish to be told of their sin. **What is sin?**

100 Jesus seeks our return to Him in confession. He loves even the most grievous sinner. Preparation for confession. Think through the Ten Commandments.

101 Future events. Prepare ourselves by constant confession. The warning. Those in serious sin will see themselves as spiritually dead. Do not be misled by the darkness of sin. Seek Jesus in the priest at confession.

103 **Satan — a real fallen angel.** People have lost the sense of sin. Cleansing of our souls. Get to confession often. The filth of our sins.

The Divine Will

Page   **Subject**

104   Have a blind trust in God. Pray for discernment. All must freely choose Jesus and accept Him as ruler of our life. Open our hearts to Jesus and give our will to Him.

105   Strive for perfection so we can live in the divine will. **To live in the divine will is to do all for Jesus every moment.** Following Jesus' will is the road to perfection.

106   Pray for guidance of the Holy Spirit. Jesus' love is warm and unconditional — follow His will. Be humble, rely on Jesus. Enter via the narrow gate.

107   Grace — our armour to fight the evil one. Follow the divine will in all things. Open our hearts to Jesus. To serve, we must conform to the divine will. In all things, strive to do the divine will to be perfect and ready for Jesus.

The Priesthood, The Mass, The Real Presence, Exposition and Morals

Page   **Subject**

109   Spiritual value of a priest. Pray for vocations. Sermons — leniency of. Lack of meaning.

110   Lack of vitality of Masses after the schism. Failure of priests to teach real presence and encourage benediction and adoration. Miracle of transubstantiation. **Encourage perpetual adoration.** Jesus' presence hidden. Have exposition frequently.

111   The Blessed Sacrament. Place of honour in the Church. Continue respect for Jesus' real presence. Promote perpetual adoration. Kneel in adoration of Jesus' presence. Need for clergy to speak out on abortion and sins of the flesh.

112   Challenge to the validity of the real presence at the Consecration. **Sacrilegious communions.** Need for confession to receive worthily. Changes following Vatican II — many were disguised lies of Satan. Need for sermons to 'cause' people to come to confession.

The Mass - Underground Masses

Page	Subject

113   **Three years suffering demonic forces.** Closure of churches. Prepare to go underground. Religious persecution — many will be misled. A time like Sodom and Gomorrah.

115   The tribulation — a battle for good and evil. Preserve a Host in a holder. Necessities — rosaries, some Hosts — one for the Monstrance. New rules of worship. Invalid Masses. Pray the Rosary and prepare.

116   **Prayer Groups: underground Masses.** The schismatic church. End of Jesus' real presence. Very few churches will remain faithful. Underground Masses — spiritual Communion. Preservation of vestments, vessels, Mass books, bread and wine. **Preserve and guard the consecrated Hosts —** evil ones will wish to desecrate them.

117   **Very few Churches will remain faithful.** Spiritual Communion. Challenge to the validity of the real presence.

118   Provision of needed vessels and unleavened bread and wine. Provide for underground Masses in prayer groups. **Gather the things for Mass** — bread, wine, books, vessels, candles. Stripping of churches. Preserve statues and crucifixes for underground Masses.

119   Churches barred from entry. Need sacramentals of rosaries, holy water, Bibles. Formal beginning of schism. Antipope's dismissal of Church tradition. Accommodation of every religion. Relaxation of laws against sins of the flesh. Banning of priests. Need for underground Masses.

Abortion

Page	Subject

120   **Abortion can be removed by prayer.** The punishment due will not go unanswered. Less regard for human life. Justification of killing. They will live to regret it. Concurrence by inaction. Stand up in public and defend Jesus' laws.

121 **The chromosome test.** All unborn babies are human. Be more vocal against abortion. The injustice of abortion demands reparation. All life is precious and to be protected. Jesus' instruction on abortion. Do not allow the evil one a victory.

122 Stand up for Jesus' commandments. Pray for mothers to relent from killing their babies. **The talents of aborted babies lost to society.** The judgement on each nation. Fight this evil.

123 Mary's request for prayer and action. Our responsibility to speak out and instruct others. The refusal to accept the unborn as human. **We are human from conception.** Abortion: a grievous sin.

125 The baptism of aborted babies — so their original sin can be forgiven. The world holocaust of abortion. Do all in your power to protest the carnage and discourage mothers.

126 The sheer numbers of those favouring abortion. Its purpose, death, can never be right. As it was in Noah's day. Heaven is in awe and disgust.

Children

Page   **Subject**

126 Ensure children are taught the faith and are led to the sacraments. The call to parents and grandparents. Children to be brought up in a loving Christian environment. The preciousness of children to Jesus. Each soul must choose Him individually. Give a good example.

Teach the children morning and night prayers and how to call on Jesus when in trouble. Teach them to read Scripture and to go to Sunday Mass. Pray for them. **Mary's promise of the scapular and the rosary.** Give them to the family. The TV babysitter. Violence and lack of morals in cartoons. Need for good influences.

129 **Bring the children to Mass whatever their age.** Teach the sacraments, forgiveness of sin, the Eucharist. Children are great imitators. They must be taught by seeing, in action, what they are to believe. Parents' responsibility for passing

on the faith. Parents' concern for the worldly — what about the spiritual??

130 Today's electronic marvels lead to the entrapment of children. Abuse by daycare providers and teachers. The need for moral values and to see the commandments being obeyed. Teach them not to receive if in mortal sin. Protect them from harm. The corruption of movies. **Take the children to Mass.** Those who refuse face the Lord's judgement.

131 Grandparents and parents watch over and protect the children. Don't stand by passively. Put scapulars on them and give them rosaries. **Home teaching of the faith: a special grace to families.** Day-care centres and schools. Parents' readiness to leave the children with others. **Take a lesser standard of living.** The deposit of faith. Children's prayers and worship on Sundays. Their spiritual welfare. Their spiritual mother and their Saviour.

132 Don't give up. Continue to pray for them. Remind them of Sunday Mass. They have to make their own decisions. Parents — spiritual guardians of the children. Show them God can help. **Prayer at mealtime and bedtime. The rosary.** Know what your children are being taught — even at college. The unknown evil influences. Encouragement by the demons of brainwashing of children. Test what they are being taught.

133 Children under the age of reason.

Suffering in Our Lives

Page   **Subject**
134 The crucifix to show Jesus' suffering. In persecution — never lose hope in Jesus' love. Jesus died for us: **we must die to ourselves to obtain salvation.** Jesus' suffering servants.
135 Jesus: still suffering for our ongoing sins. Offer all sufferings to the Father. Take up our cross daily and bear it lovingly for Jesus' Name's sake. Our purpose here is to suffer to purify our weakness to sin. **After confession: make reparation through prayer and fasting.** Offer up all suffering.
136 A lesson from Jesus in carrying our cross.

1. Confession

Volume I — Jul '93 to Jun '94

Confession at least once a month. Avoid the sin of sacrilege

P70 — **"It is good that you go to confession at least once a month or more often if you commit a mortal sin. Please avoid the sin of sacrilege.** If you have mortal sin, do not receive Communion for this is a defilement of My Sacrament."

P128 — "You must prepare for the battle with the demons with the Rosary, the cross with the corpus that you have, holy water and My Mother's scapular... Continue to keep yourself clean of soul with confession to receive My graces."

Souls in hell for sins of the flesh. Only those who ask for forgiveness can be forgiven

P144 — "I have shown [in the vision] a picture of souls being tortured in hell. I tell you more souls are going to hell for the sins of the flesh — more than any other sin.... I cannot forgive the sinner who does not ask for forgiveness. The sinner must pray to have contrition or have someone pray for them. But in the end, they must confess their sin and come to Me in repentance or face eternal damnation. This is the choice every man must make. Sin can be forgiven, but a cold heart will not find heaven."

Preparation for the warning by confession. Many souls go to hell

P210 — "Prepare for My warning. It will come when you least expect it. Be watchful and have your soul ready by frequent confession. Those in mortal sin will experience great grief at the time of the warning."

P212 — "Many people when they die, cannot believe it happened and as a result are not prepared for heaven. Many souls will go to hell because they think there is plenty of time to get spiritual later and continue on the road to worldliness. It cannot be this way for My faithful. I must be first in your lives at all times such that you are always prepared if your death should come quickly."

Go to the priest in confession. Contrition necessary

P218 — "My people, how can I receive you when I find in your soul all kinds of abominations and where it is overgrown with the debris of the world? You must first be cleansed of your sins. **Go to the priest in confession and be reconciled with Me so that you can be purified and receive My grace of life in your soul.** You must be dead in sin and not dead to Me if your soul is in mortal sin. Most important is that you have contrition for your sins. It is this willingness for forgiveness that you must keep focussed on.

"**I will forgive you, but you must be sincere to please Me.** Then your soul will be clean and tidy and I would be pleased to be with you. If you would prepare yourself to meet your King, you would not come to Me in tattered clothes. So put on your wedding garment and have your sins forgiven. Then, when you enter My banquet, all will be ready. It is important that you be watchful and ready, for you do not know the hour I will call you home to Me."

Volume II Jul '94 to Jun '95

P7 — "I await anyone who wants My graces and especially, I wait for those who seek repentance in confession. It is in being humble in asking for forgiveness that I look for in the heart of every penitent. Keep close to Me in My sacraments and continue your daily prayers to withstand the evil one."

Be sorry for your sins and Jesus will forgive them

P11 — "No matter how serious the sin, I am here for you in the Sacrament of Penance ready to heal your sins. All you need do is be sincerely sorry for your sins and I will forgive them. This is a lesson in spiritual humility, to admit your faults and ask for forgiveness. I want you to be close to Me always, so do not let sin keep any barriers between us.… All you need to do is reach out for My helping hand. Show others by your going to confession that My love waits in My sacraments for everyone. I will be among you forever."

Freedom from sin necessary for Jesus' protection

P26 — "My people, I have warned you many times to prepare for the tribulation. You must have your soul freed from sin in confession ready to receive My protection. The purification will not last long, but the three days of darkness will seem endless. You will need your blessed candles to have light.... Pray to Me always for strength and guidance through this time. You will not survive without Me."

What is sin? All sins of the flesh are mortal sins. Seek confession

P53 — "You must prepare your soul and protect it from attacks of the devil. Use your spiritual arms of Rosary, daily Mass and Communion, visits to My Blessed Sacrament and frequent confession. You must build the house of your soul on solid ground with faith as its foundation."

P65 — "You must remember that all sins of the flesh are serious mortal sins and require confession to be forgiven. They are abortion, contraception, pre-marital sex, fornication and adultery. Avoid these sins under pain of loss of My grace.... I will preach to you on confession or reconciliation since you hear little of it from your pulpits. People are still committing sin, even though they do not think so.

"I ask you to **make a monthly habit of going to confession** to receive My grace of the sacrament but most of all to ask My forgiveness of your sins. Without being sorry for your sin and admitting how it offends Me, you cannot be My disciple. Your will must come into conformity with mine if you choose to want me in heaven."

P127 — "As I have talked to you much about facing death, I want to stress to you **that living in serious sin is living a spiritual death.** This is important that you keep alive in My grace of confession. I have given you My Sacrament of Penance to be reborn through My forgiveness. Throughout your physical life, be ever attentive to stay close to me in prayer and away from serious sin."

Volume V — Oct to Dec '96

Confession — the only hope to right ourselves before the warning

P14 — "My people, you are seeing a sign of My warning which is coming soon. I am coming again to prepare My people spiritually for this event. Remember, I have told you that those with serious sin will suffer a more traumatic experience. I come, therefore, to seek your forgiveness of sin in confession. See that My Sacrament of Reconciliation is your only hope to right yourself with me before this mini-judgement. I am always here, waiting patiently for your return. If you are sorry for your sins, that is all that I am seeking.… Do not try to go through life alone, or you will be lost in your self-pride … all those who come to Me have nothing to fear.…"

P26 — "My people, I am the resurrection and the life. No one comes to heaven, unless they come through Me, for I have died that all of you may have life everlasting. Since Adam's sin, all of you have been appointed to die as a consequence of original sin. Also, you were steeped in sin and death until My resurrection. You are still weak in your sins, but now I offer you salvation by My saving power of the cross. I have ransomed you from your sins, but you must repent and seek My forgiveness in confessing your sins. Give glory and thanks to your loving God who holds out his hand to carry you all to heaven…"

Volume VIII — Jul to Sep '97

All who wish to convert will be accepted

P21 — "Every time you sin, you are like those at My scourging giving Me an extra stripe. This scene [in the vision: Jesus crucified] is to make it vivid to you how much grief each sin causes Me. I seek all of you to be sorrowful for all of your many insults to Me, and you need to seek My forgiveness in confession. Now, you need to come to Me no matter how evil you think you are. For I will accept anyone who wishes to convert and imitate My life."

P31 — "You have constant need of My cleansing graces in My Sacrament of Reconciliation. Come to Me often, so your soul can be cleansed and made radiant in My sight again. Do not wallow in your sins, but see the filth of sin around you and seek to be free. My graces are always open to you…"

Jesus will always forgive the repentant sinner. Be not afraid

P40 — "The windshield wipers [as in the vision] are symbolic of how you are cleansed and made clean [in confession]. Temptations and sin are always dropping on your windshields, but you must seek My Sacrament of Reconciliation in order to be forgiven by Me in the priest. Keep your soul always clean and in sanctifying grace and you will see clearly both at night or day… So use My Sacrament of Reconciliation to remain clean, no matter how often you call on it. I will always forgive a repentant sinner. Be not afraid of any penance you will need to do. Just come in love and I will greet you with open arms."

Sinners do not wish to be told of their sin. What is sin?

P90 — "My people, you need to be aware that **the devil is a real being. He is Lucifer, the fallen angel.** He tempts you daily to sin and you must be aware that he wants to destroy all souls on Earth. You must be conscious that people are sinning, even though they do not want either to know it or be told about it. **Sinners do not want to be told of their sins,** since they will no longer be able to have their bodily pleasures.

"For those that want sin to be revealed to them, **let me show you things some do not even think are sins.** Having intercourse before marriage; using contraception even when you are married; masturbation and any other unnatural means to prevent conception such as vasectomies and tying of the tube in women. Other sins concern ruining other's reputations with gossip, slandering others, cheating employees out of their just wages and benefits. Whenever you violate My Ten Commandments as in doing harm to your neighbour or not worshipping Me on Sundays, you need to be sorrowful for your sins and seek My forgiveness of them.

"I know you are weak and sin, but I have enabled you to return to grace through My Sacrament of Reconciliation before the priest.…"

Volume X — Jan to Mar '98

Jesus seeks our return to Him in confession. He loves even the most grievous sinners

P17 — "My people, I am asking you to return to Me in confession as the loving Father received his prodigal son. My pardon of grace awaits all those who would come to Me in seeking forgiveness of your sins. Do not be afraid to tell your sins to the priest, but think of him as Me waiting to receive you in loving embrace. Do not listen to the evil one's taunts of how you are unworthy to come to Me. I love even the most grievous sinners. So come and receive your Master's joy.

"**Do not be spiritually lazy,** but see that cleansing your sins from your soul is a necessity if you are to be saved. Those who remain in their sin and refuse My help are like those without a life preserver in the sinking boat. Come, My children, I welcome all of you into the banquet of forgiveness. All of you are sinners and need My grace of holiness in your souls. Those who have their sins cleansed are like the saints dressed in white robes ready for Me to take them to heaven."

Volume XII — Jul to Sep '98

Preparation for confession. Think through the Ten Commandments

P47 — "My people, when you come to Me in confession, you need to spend some time in contemplating your sins against Me. Do not come in haste, but think through all of My commandments so you are properly prepared. Come with a contrite heart in sorrow for your offences. Come to Me to cleanse your sins so your soul can be beautiful before me once again. Do not hold back any sins, but humbly confess everything to the priest. You need frequent confession to keep placing yourself back on the narrow road to heaven. Do not fear confession or lazily put off going, because you never know when I will call you home. Be like the wise virgins, who were prepared when the master came."

Volume XIV — Jan to Mar '99

Future events. Prepare ourselves by constant confession

P19 — "My people, I am showing you the eruption of this volcano because you are going to see an increasing frequency of these events. Each one of these eruptions has had a devastating effect on the landscape around them. The dust that they carry high into the sky will cause different colourations in the atmosphere and a dimming of the sun's light. Prepare for these events by perfecting your life in constant confession, so you will be ready for My Coming again in triumph."

The Warning: those in serious sin will see themselves as spiritually dead

P39 — "This time of My warning is getting very close and you need to have your souls prepared by frequent confession. Those found with mortal sin on their souls at the time of the warning will suffer a far more traumatic experience than those without mortal sin. Those in serious sin will see themselves as spiritually dead and face condemnation to hell if they do not change their lives."

Vol. XV — Apr to Jun '99

Do not be misled by the darkness of sin. Seek Jesus in the priest at confession

P12 — "My people, when you drive your car at night and your car lights burn out, you are cast into darkness and you are afraid to go further when you cannot see. Because you want to continue driving at night, you then rush out to replace that light so you can see again. In your soul, My grace is that same light — of faith. While you are in the state of grace, you see clearly life's road to heaven. When you are detoured into mortal sin, My light of grace is snuffed out and you become spiritually blind and it is difficult to see your way to heaven.

"Why is it that you would quickly replace your lights to see physically at night, but you fail to quickly embrace My Sacrament of Reconciliation, so you can see spiritually? Do not be misled in the darkness of your sin, but search Me out in the priest at confession, so you can renew My light in your soul. Once you have sought My forgiveness for your sins, then you can be cleansed of your sins and you will again see clearly with the eyes of faith.

You can only find the heavenly road if you are full of the light of My grace. I am the Light of the World, and I lead all of those who believe in My Name to eternal life. You cannot be renewed in your sinful life unless you come through Me. So give up your life in darkness in the love of earthly things, and exchange it for My life of love that will enlighten your soul with My Easter light."

Vol. XV — Apr to Jun '99

Satan — a real fallen angel. He encourages sin. People have lost the sense of sin

P51 — "My people, you should be aware of Satan's attacks on My churches, your families and your leaders. First of all, **Satan is a real fallen angel**. And he is encouraging sin in the world.

"This is an evil age, and it very well fits the description of Noah's day in the end times. People have lost their sense of sin and there is not enough love in your world both for Me and your neighbour. Because of this evil world, you need My help more than ever. **Come to Me in prayer and confession** and I will direct you on your way to heaven."

Vol. XV — Apr to Jun '99

Cleansing of our souls. Get to confession often. The filth of our sins

P80 — "My people, as I talked to My people in Israel of salt and lamp stands, today I am showing you this rain gutter for disposal of the water. There are many things you dispose in the trash bin, but if it was not taken away, it would inundate you and possibly cause disease. In the same way in the body if you did not flush away the toxins in your blood, you could be poisoned and die. This is true of your soul as well. **Over time you accumulate the filth of your sins which need to be cleansed or you will suffocate and die from your sins.**

"Death to the soul is more important than death to the body. The soul goes on for eternity and if you become lost in sin, you could spend forever in hell on your judgment. **So it is necessary that you get to confession often to cleanse your souls**. You cleanse the body and remove the trash. What better need do you have in cleansing your soul from sin?"

2. The Divine Will

Volume VII — Apr to Jun '97

P61 — Mary: "Once My Son, Jesus, touches your life with His everlasting peace and love, there is a whole new way of understanding your present existence. When you are part of God's oneness, serving His will is all that is important."

P79 — Jesus: "When you are one of My disciples, you must make Me an intimate part of your life. You must strive for perfection by forcing your will to walk in My divine will."

Volume II — Jul '94 to Jun '95

Have a blind trust in God. Pray for discernment

P158 — Our Lady: "When the Lord asks for your moment of truth in how you should serve Him, come forward in full trust and accept his will for you with no holding back. Take a lesson from Zechariah and have no doubt or disbelief. Also, as Ahaz, do not make excuses or try to put off the Lord for your own designs. Have a blind trust in your God and He will see your sincerity and bless you with His gifts.

"If you should decide to do your own will, you will see how a dismal failure lies in wait for you. You cannot achieve His will for you without your acceptance. You must pray for discernment, how to follow what He wills for you. You will never be disappointed if you let Him lead you. You will see, your yes will be your most thankful decision."

All must freely choose Jesus and accept Him as ruler of our life

P201 — "You must all be purified of the desires of earthly things.... My warning is offering you a choice as I have mentioned before. Choose Me or the world. Do not worry about your relatives. Pray for them to choose wisely and all will be treated equally. All must freely choose Me and accept Me if they are to be saved.... If you do not accept Me as ruler of your life, you cannot enter My Kingdom."

Volume III — Jul '95 to Jun '96

Open our hearts to Jesus and give our will to Him

P8 — "It is each person, as I have told you, that restricts My love. You must open your hearts to Me, so I can use you as My instruments. It is only when you give your will over to Me, that I can mould you to do My will. You must have an unquestioning faith and hope in all I do for you."

P18 — "My dear children, I am asking you to have an open mind and heart to My word. Only if you are open to receive Me, can you hear My voice. Many want to be in control of their lives in every aspect, but I call on you to give up your will to Me so that I may lead you, and you will be more in step with My plan for each of you."

Volume IV — Jul to Sep '96

Strive for perfection so we can live in the divine will

P79 — "Never lose sight of following My will in what you do each day. Your daily prayers are testimony for your everlasting love for Me. Keep close to Me through confession, prayer and your acts of mercy. Strive, My people, to be one with Me in perfection, so you can live with Me in the divine will."

Volume V — Oct to Dec '96

To live in the divine will is to do all for Jesus every moment

P45 — "Give your will over to Me, if you are to seek perfection... You must train your body to be in conformance with a joyful soul which is on Me only. Seek to live in the divine will which means doing everything for Me at every moment of the day. Come to Me with this love in your heart, and I will remould you into an acceptable, beautiful soul to be presented to My Father in heaven. Continue now in your daily devotions and keep close to Me in front of My Blessed Sacrament and in Holy Communion. I am the power of your life and all your gifts come from Me."

Volume VIII — Jul to Sep '97

Following Jesus' Will is the road to perfection. Pray for guidance of the Holy Spirit

P9 — "What does it gain you, to have acquired the whole world and then lose your soul? It is important to keep everything in perspective. I give you many gifts in this life to help you and your neighbour, but do not live for these things only. You need to see that following My will is your only road to perfection. Consecrate your whole life to Me and I will provide for your every need."

P31 — "When you use your eyes of faith, it is the spiritual context that puts life in full perspective. Learn to view things more as I would see them and you will gain in perfection.
Pray each day to be guided by the Holy Spirit **in your actions and you will be able to follow My will for you. It is this direction of following My divine will that will truly show you how to follow the light…**"

P44 — "Now, I beg you to take up your daily cross and carry it for the sake of My love. I give you many gifts in this world. This is the one favour that I ask in return, that you follow My will even in suffering. I had to suffer and die for all of your sins…"

Jesus' love is warm and unconditional — follow His will

P67 — "I am even pursuing you to your dying breath in order to save your souls from Satan and from being lost in hell. I have shown you in My death for you, how much I love you. This love of mine is warm and unconditional. All I ask, is that you love Me and follow My will for you."

P71 — "The price of eternal life is worth giving up everything of this world, including your own will. You should be willing to seek My divine will so that nothing can come between you and Me. When you follow Me with this reservation, truly the Kingdom of Heaven will be opened to you."

P84 — "My people, you must be willing to suffer with Me each day and endure the hardships that befall you. When you reach out to Me for help, I will be walking with you as you carry your cross… live your life following My will and look to Heaven for your enjoyment.… You can only gain Heaven if you pick up your cross and bear it lovingly for Me. Give Me your burdens, and I will lighten your loads."

Be humble, rely on Jesus. Enter via the narrow gate

P90 — "You may be knowledgeable in some things, but you must become like little children if you are to enter into heaven. Practice being humble, and rely only on My help to lead you through life. Being a fool for Me in the eyes of the world takes courage in the abuse you may undergo. Those spiritual things of value and the virtues you need to reach Heaven take time and work to develop. Enter the narrow gate in full submission to the Divine will, and you will win the greatest prize that your soul could desire — eternal life with Me in Heaven."

P92 — "You cannot overpower the devil on your own. There you are dealing with angels who have more power than you can ever have by yourself. You must rely on My help to get you through life. I will not force My help on you. As in life, see that My ways are better than your ways in leading you to spiritual perfection. I am here always willing to help you. See the light and humble yourselves by letting your will conform to My divine will. By accepting that My plan is better for you, you will be able to advance spiritually as well."

Volume X — Jan to Mar '98

Grace — our armour to fight the evil one. Follow the divine will in all things

P2/3 — "During life, My grace gives you the armour to fight the evil one. Each day you must go out and do battle to witness to My Name and My love for all men. Defend your faith against all who would defile Me and stand up in public to be counted as one of My faithful. Be proud of your heritage in My promise and follow My Will in all that you do. By testifying to My divine will, you gain your crown of eternal life with Me."

Volume XII — Jul to Sep '98

Open our hearts to Jesus. To serve, we must conform to the divine will

P18 — "I call on you many times to come to Me in the innocence of children. It is in the simple life that you will see to put away the cares of the world and be focussed on following My will. Open your heart to Me so I can enter it and show you how to live in My divine will. Do not let pride run your life…"

P29 — "My people, remember that you are here to serve and not be served. By your seeking fame and riches on this earth, you only seek to serve your own will. In reality, you all were created in My image to know, love and serve Me. When you serve Me, you have to conform your will to following My divine will…"

Volume XIV — Jan to Mar '99

In all things, strive to do the divine will to be perfect and ready for Jesus

P49 — "My people, this vision of the stairway is to represent your way to heaven. The white rug symbolises the wedding feast that I am calling you to. The colour white also means that you have to be purified with the proper garments to come to heaven. In all of your actions and deeds you must strive to live My divine will in order to be perfect and ready to greet Me. Use My sacraments, especially Reconciliation, to prepare your souls for Me."

3. The Priesthood, the Mass, the Real Presence, Exposition and Morals

Volume VIII — Jul to Sep '97

P8/9 — "My dear priest-sons, it is not easy to deal with all of the many thoughts of those in a local parish. There are many interests and desires of those wishing to have their way in My Church. **It is most important that My priests be spiritual leaders in their own congregations.** Even though it is easier to go along with a majority opinion, it is more important to be willing to hold up My Gospel teachings as the more appropriate way of life. **Do not be afraid to stand up for the teachings of My true Church, even when it is not popular.** My priests are to represent Me on Earth, so be daring to preach as I would preach.

"Do not be so worried about the collection box as you should be concerned about saving souls under your care. To feed your people properly, be willing to bring the people closer to the sacraments for their spiritual strength. **When occasions arise, speak out on the problems of the lack of morals of this day.** Speak out to wake them up to their sins and how they need to be forgiven in confession. Those priests, who truly imitate My life in prayer and duty, will find true love in following My will."

Volume III — Jul '95 to Jun '96

Spiritual value of a priest. Pray for vocations

P197 — "My people, as you watch your priest offer My Body and Blood at the consecration of the Mass, be thankful that you can receive My intimate presence. The spiritual value of a priest has a value you do not even realise. This is why it is so important to pray for vocations and help your priests. They dispense My sacraments daily, but look what would happen if they were not there [as in the vision]. You need My priests for your spiritual nourishment. Even though many Catholics are lukewarm to Me, be ever thankful you have this treasure of Myself present through the priests. I love you and I have instituted these gifts of mine for your benefit."

Sermons — leniency of. Lack of meaning

P209 — "My people, I am showing you what happens when men lose trust and faith in Me. Gradually, you will see the priests become so lenient in their sermons that their words will fall over themselves with no meaning. If My priests cannot stand behind the Gospel and uphold My ways, instead of their own, then what little faith they have, will be lost. It is this rejection of leading My people to Me and not abandoning their ways, that will bring down My traditions, as you know them."

Lack of validity of Masses after the schism

"When this schism occurs, I will remove My blessing and there will no longer be valid Masses, as their faith will become hollow. It is at that time in the tribulation that evil use of My churches will be confounded, and you will need to seek underground Masses. My remnant faithful will then lead My true Church and preserve My presence. Pray, My people, to endure this starvation of My sacraments. You will then have only your rosaries and occasional Masses to sustain you."

Volume VII — Apr to Jun '97

Failure of priests to teach real presence and encourage benediction and adoration

P32 — "Some of My priest-sons are at fault for not teaching My real presence and are not encouraging benediction or perpetual adoration. If you cannot find time to adore Me and give thanks, how are you going to find time to be saved and seek My forgiveness. These signs of My rejection and lack of reverence are again showing you the apostasy that is already abound. Come to Me at the Mass and your prayer groups and I will unite My remnant to do spiritual battle with those evil people who are denying Me."

Miracle of transubstantiation. Encourage perpetual adoration

P57 — "Believe, My faithful, that I am truly present in the consecrated bread and wine. You have witnessed many miracles of My real blood coming forth from the Host as evidence to those unbelievers. I tell you, at every Mass you witness My miracle in the transubstantiation when the bread and wine are made into My body and blood. Take advantage of this time to adore Me in exposition of My Host, for a time is coming when this privilege will be taken away. I recommend to all of you to encourage your priests to have perpetual adoration of My Host. I bring many graces to those who can visit Me and give Me praise and adoration. Even if you can have only one hour, one day or the daylight hours. Any time you can have adoration will bring many blessings on your Church and the people of your area."

Volume VIII — Jul to Sep '97

Jesus' Presence hidden. Have Exposition frequently

P33 — "It is right to give My Blessed Sacrament a place of honour, but many churches have hid My presence that many cannot see where it is. You also should remember that My Blessed Sacrament is meant to be adored. Encourage your clergy to have exposition frequently to share the many graces the people can have by even visiting My exposed Host. Also give Me adoration and acknowledge My love as often as possible. You have the Kingdom of God present among you in My real presence. Give thanks to God for all the blessings that have been bestowed upon you."

The Blessed Sacrament. Place of Honour in the Church

P52 — "My people, I am grateful to all who give Me reverence in My Blessed Sacrament. It is important to remember to give honour and praise to Me and not just the traditions.… You should give My Blessed Sacrament proper respect by having it in a place of honour in My Church. When you come to Church, you come to respect Me, not just the altar. Those that belittle confession and prayer are doing my people more of a disservice. It is important to seek My forgiveness of your sins at all times. Those who do not speak of sin and the forgiveness of sin are avoiding their duty to save souls. See that bringing souls to Me is the most significant thing you can do while you are on Earth. It is this battle to save souls that is what life is all about."

Continue respect for Jesus' real presence. Promote perpetual adoration

P64 — "My people, you are to do everything in your power to continue respect for My real presence in the bread and wine. Even though some may not believe in My real presence, I am still there. **The more you can promote perpetual adoration, the more blessings will be on your parish.** Those who adore Me and give Me time out of their busy schedules will be rewarded in the hereafter."

Kneel in Adoration in Jesus' presence

P71 — "My people, when you come to Me in prayer, it would help you to kneel in adoration. **When you pray on your knees,**

you can be more disposed to Me and avoid distractions. Pray from your heart and keep focussed on a statue or picture of Me. Those who come to Me with prayers of adoration or mercy for sinners have chosen the better portion."

Need for clergy to speak out on abortion and sins of the flesh

P100 — "It is My Pope who is most vocal on sin and repentance. The bishops and priests of your day, for the most part, are not speaking out about sin, conversion, and a return to confession. Look at the messages coming forth from the visionaries that I send before you. My mother and I are constantly encouraging prayer and preparation for My coming again. Many clergy are afraid to speak out on the evils of your day as abortions and sins of the flesh, since they fear the loss of donations from people who would be upset."

Volume X — Jan to Mar '98

Challenge to validity of real presence at the consecration

P8 — "My people, your Mass is under siege from the evil one. Many are trying to implement changes in the Mass that strike at the sacred. Different species of bread and different words throughout the Mass are challenging the validity of My real presence at the Consecration. The words I gave My apostles were My model for My Eucharistic Banquet. **Those who do not say the proper words are not saying valid Masses.** All that is sacred at Mass must be preserved or you are just going through the motions with no meaning."

Sacrilegious Communions. Need for confession to receive worthily

P55 — "My people, you have become too relaxed in your worship at Mass and you give My real presence little respect. You must struggle to preserve the proper words of the Mass, especially those of the Consecration. Also, many are receiving Holy Communion in mortal sin which is a sin of sacrilege against My Body and Blood of this sacrament. Your souls must be properly purified by confession or in a state of grace in order to receive your Lord in Holy Communion."

Volume XIII — Oct to Dec '98

Changes following Vatican II — Many were disguised lies of Satan

P47 — "My people, I am showing how many changes have been brought in because of the spirit of Vatican II, but really were disguised *lies* from Satan. These errors and the loss of reverence were brought to you as a 'good' but they were like a Trojan Horse, reflecting your times."

Need for sermons to 'cause' people to come to confession

P48 — "It is important to see how your local priests have been duped by Satan and those urging 'changes.' The priests have become weak in feeding My souls. They should be encouraging Confession rather than worrying about their time spent in the confessional. If only a few come, it is because **there are no sermons on sin** to cause the parishioners to seek the Sacrament of Reconciliation."

P49 — **"Tell the people, My priests, of the serious sins of the flesh that are sending more souls to hell.** Speak out against abortion, birth control, masturbation and fornication without worrying of 'offending' people of their sins. My priests should be stressing how to live chaste and pure lives. At the priests' judgements they will have to answer in part for not making their parishioners obey My Fifth and Sixth Commandments.

Pray for your priests that they may have the courage and faith to support the truths of My apostles and My Pope."

4. The Mass — Underground Masses

Volume I — Jul '93 to Jun '94

Three years suffering demonic forces. Church closures. Prepare to go underground

P27 — "You will suffer through demonic forces for three and a half years. The faithful will be forced underground like the catacombs. Some will be martyred, but fear not, for I will strengthen and protect My little ones. In the end, My Sacred Heart will triumph."

P45 — "Your churches and Masses you will not have much longer. For the demons will grow in strength and eventually force the churches to close. At that time you may have underground Masses for a while, until the priests are also found. In the end of the evil age you will huddle together to say your rosaries — this will be your only weapon against evil...."

P131 — "You must **prepare and go underground** to avoid this evil time. You must pray and ask for My guidance as to what to do. Do not fear, I will allow you to endure this test with My graces. So continue your prayers to understand that My ways are not your ways."

Religious Persecution — Many will be misled. A time like Sodom and Gomorrah

P181 — "Prepare for your future religious persecution. Many people will be misled in their faith on beliefs which are heresy to Me. The religious leaders will let their pride mislead them and their people. You will at first have to seek out underground Masses to avoid the heretical teachings. Then there will be confrontations, and they will try to ban you from your churches for believing in My faith. The people of this time will allow the demons to cause them all perversions of sex and drugs. It will be much like Sodom and Gomorrah in Lot's time.

"This is why My judgement must come again with fire to purify the earth. It will be so perverted that it will require My intervention to bring peace once again to the earth. **There will only be a small remnant left to preach the Gospel.** You will be honoured to keep your faith through these trials. Pray for strength now that you can endure this test of evil."

P224 — "My people, in a short time your churches will no longer be My place of Mass. Yea, it will soon be a time of persecution instead. Relish the joy of My service and receiving Me freely now since not long and you will be at an underground service. You will be in hiding from the authorities as I have previously advised you. In My time of persecution My faithful ones will be tried as never before in history. The evil one and his agents will seek you out to torture and kill you. Do not be afraid, I will protect you from the evil one's attempts."

Volume II — Jul '94 to Jun '95

The tribulation — a battle of good and evil. Preserve a Host in a holder

P36 — "My people, soon you will approach the tribulation which will indeed be a battle of good and evil.... You will no longer be able to find Me in the churches since the evil one's agents will attack them. If you are fortunate, you may find Me in underground Masses. If you can preserve a Host in a holder, you can protect My presence from desecration. You may then carry Me around in hiding to give hope and joy to the faithful..."

P176 — "My people, during the tribulation you will be most ecstatic to have a Mass where the priest could consecrate some Hosts."

Necessities — Rosaries, some hosts, one for the monstrance

"This will be another of your necessities to take with your rosaries — that is, some hosts and one for your monstrance. Once in these times, it will be good to keep Me in a holder to bolster your spiritual strength. During your trial, with Me sacramentally in your midst, you could draw on My love at an appropriate time. Be prepared, My children. As you will see events lead up quickly to the times of persecution."

Volume III — Jul '95 to Jun '96

New rules of worship: Invalid masses. Pray the rosary and prepare

P247 — "... My faithful will need underground Masses wherever a priest may be found. As the imposter pope takes control, you will see, those that follow him will be mislead. By his new rules of worship, even the Masses will be made invalid. My people, pray your rosaries and prepare for this time, for you will have to seek Me in secret, and to avoid any services under the control of this evil pope."

Volume VII — Apr to Jun '97

P55 — "My people, you will find Me at the breaking of the bread at the Mass. Come to the Mass wherever you can have one, and I will be present among you. Know all of you present today, that I will never abandon you. Even if you must come to underground Masses, come, that you may see and preserve My presence in your midst. Seek Me and you will find Me…"

Importance of Prayer Groups

P85 — "My people, I am showing you how you will have to pray for your priests when it comes time to decide whether or not to stay with John Paul II and the remnant Church. Your prayer groups will be important, for this is where you will have your underground Masses."

Volume VIII — Jul to Sep '97

The schismatic church. End of Jesus' real presence

P72 — "Do not give any allegiance to this next pope who will blaspheme Me by worshiping the Antichrist. When you see this evil pope deviate from the teaching of My revelation, you will know that it is the beginning of the end of My schismatic Church. My true faithful will be forced into underground Masses. Your current places of worship will soon become corrupt in their practices. When the priests change the proper consecration, My real presence will no longer be there. Pray for spiritual strength during this coming trial of the tribulation."

Volume IX — Oct to Nov '97

Preservation of vestments, vessels, Mass books, bread & wine

P34 — "My people, it is time to prepare now for your underground Masses. Go now and obtain all of the vessels, vestments and books to say Mass. Stock up on your bread and wine.

"There is coming a time very shortly when you will no longer have your churches for Mass. The schismatic church will take them over and soon there will no longer be any valid Masses there."

Preserve and guard the Consecrated Hosts

"You will need to find a faithful priest for a true Mass of My real presence. You will have to preserve and guard My Consecrated Hosts from the evil ones who will desire them to desecrate."

"I will be close to you during this persecution. Call on Me for spiritual communion when you cannot get to a valid Mass. I love you, My people. Remain faithful to Me even if you must suffer for My name's sake."

Very few Churches will remain faithful. Spiritual communion

P85 — "Very few Churches will be faithful to My traditions as time goes on. Is it any wonder that they will even welcome the Antichrist as a man of peace? Do not be discouraged, My faithful, but do not lose your fervour for My true presence. If you cannot have valid Masses, you may have to go to underground Masses with holy priests. You may eventually have to pray for Spiritual communion when My angels will deliver you My real presence in the manna. Preserve your faith and never let anyone try to steal you away to an unfaithful sheepfold."

Volume X — Jan to Mar '98

Challenge to the validity of the Real Presence

P8 — "My people, your Mass is under siege from the evil one. Many are trying to implement changes in the Mass that strike at the sacred. Different species of bread and different words throughout the Mass are challenging the validity of My real presence at the Consecration. The words I gave My apostles were My model for My Eucharistic Banquet. Those who do not say the proper words are not saying valid masses. All that is sacred at Mass must be preserved or you are just going through the motions with no meaning."

P12 — "My people, when the schism comes to the churches, you will be forced into the underground church. Those who stay at the schismatic churches will have to discern for themselves when they need to leave. As continuing changes occur in the Mass and when My traditions are violated, there will come a point when their meetings will not have My presence. Those who go into underground Masses will be in preparation for the Antichrist's power. Those in the schismatic churches will gradually see their churches closed or burned by the Antichrist and his agents. They will not know which way to turn, but My remnant will already have been

117

prepared for this religious persecution. My remnant will suffer in the wilderness, but I will protect you from the evil ones.

"You will share My Eucharistic Presence with My holy remnant priests. It is then that you are to preserve My Host in the monstrance for all to worship.

"I will not leave you without My Eucharistic Presence until the end of time. I will be faithful in helping you throughout the time of the tribulation. Keep your hope and love for Me in your heart before My Sacred Host"

Provision of needed vessels and unleavened bread and wine

P100 — "My people, you will soon be tested by a schism in My Church where your churches will be taken over by those against Pope John Paul II. This is why I am preparing My remnant to support those priests who will still follow the true teachings of My Church.

"You must prepare now so you can provide places in your prayer groups for underground Masses. Provide the needed vessels and the unleavened bread and wine. The later stages of persecution will come as many of your churches will be destroyed or used for other purposes."

Volume XI Apr to Jun '98

Gather the things for Mass — bread, wine, books, vessels, candles

P47 — "My people, again I am asking you to gather your things for the Mass. You will need bread, wine, books, vessels and candles.

"You would be advised to befriend a priest loyal to Me that would have a place to stay. Celebrate Mass as long as you can. Then you will have to carry My Consecrated Host from place to place to preserve My true presence among you. You will realise how precious the Mass is when it will be difficult to attend one."

Stripping of churches. Preserve statues and crucifixes

P78 — **The vision:** ... *I could see holes in the floor of a Church and then a scene of a Church stripped of all the statues, altars and pews. Jesus said:* "My people ... the next test will be the evil people, who will be secretly undermining your churches. They will gradually strip your churches of kneelers, statues and crosses all in the name of renewal and modernism. Even My tabernacles are hidden in rooms away from the main body of the church so that it will be hard to find. Why are you allowing these evil people to remove the traditions of your past? These churches will become so devoid of anything holy that they will become just a shell of a building."

Preserve the statues and crucifixes for your underground Masses.

"As religious persecution will increase, you will have to hold your Masses in secret. Eventually, you will have to go into hiding away from the Antichrist's agents who will try to kill you...."

Volume XII — Jul to Sep '98

Barred from entry to churches. Need sacramentals of rosaries, holy water, Bibles

P38 — "My people, a time is coming when your churches will be barred from entry, as you will suffer a religious persecution. No longer will you be able to share Mass openly in public. For a while you will have underground Masses, which you should prepare for even now. As the tribulation proceeds, even a secret Mass will be hard to find... you will need your sacramentals of rosaries, holy water and your Bibles..."

Volume XIV — Jan to Mar '99

Formal beginning of the Schism. Antipope's dismissal of Church traditions

P29 — "My people, I have been warning you of the coming schism in My Church, but it will come as no surprise to you. You already have many divisions in My Church, which are apparent in those who do not follow My Pope son, John Paul II. **When this current Pope is exiled, your schism will formally begin.**

"**The next pope will be an Antipope,** who will dismiss many of My Church's long-standing traditions and laws. This evil 'pope' will accommodate every religion, and will relax the laws against the sins of the flesh. By his evil decrees, you will know of his evil intent to try to destroy My Church. When he promotes the Antichrist, there will be no doubt in anyone's mind of the evil nature of this imposter 'pope'.

"Fear not, My faithful, for I will raise up My remnant Church to carry on My valid real presence. It will be My loyal priests and bishops that will carry on My underground Church. I will still be among you, supporting your souls, even amidst the tribulation. I will strengthen you in this time to endure the trial of the Antichrist."

P78 — "My people, you should treasure every opportunity to go to Mass and share with Me in Holy Communion. At every Mass you give witness to a miracle of My changing the bread and wine into My Body and My Blood.

"There will come a day when it will be difficult to find a priest to say Mass. The priests will be banned from the churches during the tribulation, so there will only be underground Masses at that time. But I will not leave you alone. As you call on Me in spiritual communion, I will have your angels give you My Heavenly Manna, so you will always have My real presence among you. This will require full trust in Me to leave your things behind and let My angels lead you to My safe havens."

5. Abortion

Volume I — Jul '93 to Jun '94

Abortion can be removed by prayer. The punishment due will not go unanswered

P32 — Our Lady of Guadalupe: "Your country continues to persecute the unborn. I say to you **if enough prayers are said, I will remove abortion from your land.**"

P96 — "You will first be tested as a country by severe ravages from the elements. Man has not acknowledged a connection between his sin and apathy to Me with the extremes in the weather. I will indeed make it known to him. The punishment due for the sins of abortion will not go unanswered. Later you will experience even worse events which I will tell you beforehand."

Volume II — Jul '94 to Jun '95

Less regard for human life. Justification of killing. They will live to regret it

P140 — "Many have noticed how the number of killings have increased in your streets. As you see an ongoing number of abortions continue, your society is witnessing less regard for the value of human life. This is how evil suggestions allow people to justify killing in their warped minds where nothing is sacred..."

P164 — "Your killing of innocent unborn children continues to this day unabated... Do you not realise that each of their angels witness to Me in this slaughter? **Do you think the injustice of this killing will go unanswered?** I tell you, all nations who participate in abortion will live to regret their actions. Those who would harm innocent children, would be better that a millstone be cast around their neck and then they should be thrown into the ocean. For their punishment lies before them. Even if forgiven, they must suffer some retribution for their offence to My plans."

Concurrence by inaction. Stand up in public and defend Jesus' laws

P186 — "I tell you law-makers and judges will be held accountable twice as much for being able to overturn these laws [permitting abortion] and doing nothing to stop it. You people are concurring in this act of killing by your inaction and will also be held liable. **Unless you are willing in public to stand up and defend My laws, I will not witness for you before My Father.** You must be more active in deed and prayer to try and bring this injustice to an end. You will be seeing more chastisements for not heeding My words. I will continue to bring you to your knees until you acknowledge My law and My will. I love you, My people, but justice must be done."

Volume III — Jul '95 to Jun '96

The chromosome test. All unborn babies are human. Be more vocal against abortion

P309 — "My people, I am showing you these chromosomes, so that you will realise that all of these unborn babies are fully human and made in My likeness. See to it that you respect life's right to exist, without killing your babies in the womb. Pray, My people, that you increase your love for Me, by being more vocal against abortion and doing what you can to help those with problem pregnancies... If you do not stop this abomination in abortion, your civilisation will slowly die for lack of replacement. Treasure new life and protect them from the butchers who seek to profit from this blood money."

Volume IV — Jul to Sep '96

The injustice of abortion demands reparation. All life is precious and to be protected

P27 — "...This injustice in the killing of My little ones demands much reparation for this sin. There is even more judgement coming, since you do not even recognise the evil in your daily abortions. Once life is set in motion, it is precious and should be protected in all its forms. When you violate My creations, you demand punishment from My justice... Those evil doers, who do not repent, will be cast into the eternal flames of My wrath in hell."

Jesus' instruction on how to deal with abortion. All life is precious. Do not allow the evil one a victory

P31 — "My people, I wish to instruct you in how to deal with those able to understand the issue of abortion. Many times I have asked you to pray for these potential mothers, that they see the value and preciousness of life far and above any reason to destroy even one life. So, also, you must deal with those that may not desire an abortion, but they are tolerant of women who wish to kill their growing babies. Think of how abhorrent it was for a woman to drown her children and how she was tried for murder. Is it any less serious at which point in life that someone would take a life? **All life is precious to Me whether it be an adult or a growing baby in the womb.** If you could prevent someone from committing murder, would you not do it, no matter whether you would offend peoples' feelings or not?

"Stand up for Jesus' commandments. Pray for mothers to relent from killing their babies.

"It is important, My friends, to advise your people that if your abortions are not stopped, My hand of wrath will come upon you. **Remind them of My justice with Noah, Sodom and Gomorrah and Nineveh.** You will meet a similar fate, unless you fight against this killing. Do not allow the evil one a victory in your killings because you were too lazy or afraid to stand up for my commandments against murder."

P48 — **The vision:** *I could see some old blackboards and baby cribs discarded in part of a junk yard. Jesus said:* "My people, I am showing you this scene because the little babies, that you are killing, will never get to use these cribs or experience going to school. See the importance of stopping these abortions, so these loves I have given a plan may come to fulfillment. Do not thwart the life I have given, but avoid this sin of abortion. Pray for these mothers, that they will relent from killing their babies. Show them the true value of life by your evangelization."

The talents of aborted babies lost to society. The judgement on each nation. Fight this evil

P50"My people… think of how I have endowed each person from birth with individual talents for their life's mission… If you become lazy and do not fulfill your use of My talents, you will have to account for such waste at the judgement… Another waste of My gifts and talents is seen in your killing of the babies in abortion. **These killed babies had certain talents that they were not permitted to carry out,** and your society will not benefit from their skills as a result.

"Not only is it a loss to you, but it thwarts My plan for their lives in how they would have made their contributions to life. This sin of abortion, therefore, wears heavy on the judgement of each nation that permits abortion. See how many afflictions of problems and chastisements that are coming down on you as a result. Fight this evil with prayer and any of your talents that you can use to turn back this tide of sin."

Mary's request for prayer and action. Our responsibility to speak out and instruct others

P59 — Mary said: "…I wish to direct your prayers to stopping abortion in your country. My tears are flowing now and the statues are weeping for the killing of these babies. My Son is very displeased with this disregard for life as well.

"**Many of your chastisements have been coming for this, more than any other sin.** You have leaders in this fight against abortion. I am asking your prayers and your public witness against these sins of abortion. Both prayer and action are most powerful in this battle. If you do not speak out against this evil, you will be held responsible for your inaction. When God's laws are violated so blatantly, it is your duty to instruct your brothers and sisters of their errors."

Volume V — Oct to Dec '96

The refusal to accept the unborn as human. We are human from conception. Abortion a grievous sin

P27 — "My people ... It is bad enough that you are killing your babies, but still your society has yet to accept that they are even human. When you declare it a human at birth, at which point in your own development do you consider yourselves less than human? You are human from conception, since you came from human parents. Your society denies the unborn is human, so it can justify taking their lives.

"**This killing is a grievous sin,** and it becomes a sin against the spirit, even more so, when you refuse to accept it as a sin of murder. If you are to be saved, these sins must be confessed and forgiven. Even many women suffer from their guilt, since deep down they sense a guilt from their loss of their unborn children.... **If you fail to seek My forgiveness or rationalise it as not a sin, you will be condemned at the judgement.** It is this attitude of abortion acceptance that calls down My wrath on your nation."

P90 — Mary said: "My dear children, you remember the Scripture passage '...and Rachel was weeping for her children because they are no more.' You are approaching the feast of those holy innocents that died at the hands of Herod. Now, in your own world, innocent life is still being taken by abortion, but you mothers are not weeping for the loss of your children. Wake up and see the blood on your hands and pray to stop this ruthless killing of babies. Life is too precious to snuff it out with no regard. Pray for these mothers to stop killing their babies."

Volume VI — Jan to Mar '97

The baptism of aborted babies — so their Original Sin can be forgiven

P75 — "My people, I call your attention to your many abortions which share their brief life with you. Another facet of abortion is that very few of the aborted babies are ever baptised. The reason for this is that most of the mothers do not even want to recognise that there is human life there. I tell you, since the conception of these babies, **life can only be instilled by placing the souls in that single cell.** Those having abortions do not even think there is a soul present.

"This lack of reverence for a life being present weighs heavily on these mothers. By not recognising life, they fail to baptise these small babies. Even these mothers I will forgive their sin if they are sorry for their sin and come to Me for forgiveness. **Encourage all mothers to baptise their infants, so the baby's Original Sin can be forgiven.** Pray much for these mothers, for their spiritual freedom hangs in the balance."

Volume XIV - Jan to Mar '99

The world holocaust of abortion

P21 — "My people, you are appalled to think of the martyrdom of a young girl as in today's St. Agnes... You should be equally appalled at all of the little lives being martyred by your sins of abortion. Not only is this holocaust evident in your own country [the USA], **but it is even worse in the rest of the world.** In some countries abortion is at such a rate as to even threaten the decrease in population. You have become so obsessed at controlling your family sizes, that you do not care about these atrocities against Me. Do all in your power to protest the carnage and discourage mothers. You have been upset with the brutal killings of Kosovo, yet why do you have no feelings for the millions of My babies you kill every day? Because you do not always see these little bodies destroyed, you have put it out of your mind. Think of the filled garbage cans and other ways these babies are used for cosmetics and you know why My justice is coming soon to condemn you. Do everything in your power to protest this carnage and discourage these mothers from committing these mortal sins, of killing, against Me."

12 August 1999

The sheer number of those favouring abortion. Its purpose is death and can never be right

"My people, many times you are overwhelmed by the sheer numbers of people supporting abortion. This struggle to stop abortion has seemed futile against monied people in favour of population control. Do not despair that you are only one voice against many. You know that truth is on your side and that killing of infants in the womb is wrong in My eyes for any reason. So be strong in your resolve to stand up for your faith and My commandments. Abortion's purpose is death and it can never be rightfully advocated in My sight."

16 September 1999

As it was in Noah's day. Heaven is in awe and disgust

"My people, this vision shows you how the stench of your sins is rising to Heaven in witness of your offences against Me. Your killings, abortions, and sins of the flesh have become so rampant that you have reached the time as it was in Noah's day. My justice is calling out for My wrath against those who are sinning with no contrition for their actions. Heaven is in awe and disgust of your disregard for My glory and your abomination of sin...."

6. Children

Volume I — Jul '93 to Jun '94

Ensure children are taught the faith and are led to the sacraments

P51 — "Send the children to Me, for I love them in My presence. You are all the caretakers of My little ones who are so precious to Me. See to it that they are taught the faith and are led to the

sacraments. You must come to Me as children with childlike faith
— without worrying about how men will think of you. But woe to
those who abuse or mislead My children, for they will pay severely...."

Volume II — Jul '94 to Jun '95

The call to parents and grandparents. Children to be brought up in a loving Christian environment

P68 — Mary said: "...I, as your spiritual mother, am asking
each parent and even grandparents to watch over these precious
little ones. It is up to you to see that they receive a Christian upbringing so that they will be acquainted with My Son. In many
cases you must direct them back to Church or pray for their conversions. These are your charges, your responsibilities since you
helped bring them into the world. You are called to be apostles, but
your own relatives should receive your first attention. My Son loves
the children and wants them brought up in a loving Christian environment which you can provide."

P305 — "...Now, even more, it is important that you help the
little children to learn the true faith. These little lives can be formed
around Me or can be misled to follow the things of earth. It is
important by your example to show them the need for God in their
lives. It becomes imperative to show them before the time when
the evil one's influence will spread. Pray much, for My children,
and let the children pray with you...."

Volume III — Jul '95 to Jun '96

The preciousness of children to Jesus. Each soul must choose Him individually. Give a good example

P11 — "My dear people, I send you many young souls, both
through your children and your grandchildren. You must understand how precious each of these lives are to Me. I trust them in
your care, that you all must work to pass the faith down to each of
them. You have a heavy responsibility for their souls. You need to
direct them and teach them how to lead good Christian lives. Each
soul must choose Me individually, but it is their upbringing in fol-

lowing the commandments which will have the biggest influence on their spiritual lives. They look to you for guidance and example.

"My children, if some of your family should be led astray, pray for them, that they may be inspired to return to the faith. Be a continual beacon of faith and hope for all your relatives, since you do not realise how much they get their faith strength from you."

P290 — "… parents and grandparents have a responsibility for the spiritual welfare of each child in your influence… From their infancy, teach them how to pray, especially morning and night prayers. Teach them how to call on Me when they have troubles… **Show the children how to read Scripture and how to go to Mass on Sunday.** It is this good upbringing that will bring these souls to Me and keep yourselves on the right path as well. Pray for these souls and encourage them to God, so when you meet Me at the judgement, you will have met your duty to Me."

Volume IV — Jul to Sep '96

Mary's promise of the scapular and the Rosary. Give the scapular to family members and others

P6 — Mary said: "My dear children…I have given you my promise that if you wear my scapular and follow my Rosary, you will not face the flames of hell. Give my scapular to all your family members and those who want to be saved and I will watch over them. Take advantage of these blessings and you will have nothing to fear in the afterlife."

The TV babysitter. Too much violence and lack of moral character in cartoons. The need for good influences

P27 — "My people, I wish to give you a message for protecting My little ones. Too often in your society of electronics, you have allowed the TV to become your babysitter. Many children are watching programming without any care from their parents as to what they are viewing. Most of the cartoons and some other programs are not proper examples to impressionable children. Know exactly what your children are watching or leave the TV turned off. Even in the cartoons there is much violence and poor moral character portrayed… See to it that your children have only good influences around them, or you may not understand how they can turn so violent. If they are taught violence and are around violence in the home, this may form deep effects on their future behaviour. Pray for your children…"

Bring the children to Mass whatever their age. Teach the sacraments, forgiveness of sin, the Eucharist

P42 — "My people, look to your young children that you instill the flame of faith in them by your example. Do not let any of My little ones wander in your bringing them up. See they are brought to Mass on Sunday no matter what their age. Teach them the sacraments especially, the forgiveness of sin in confession and the reception of Me in My Eucharist at the proper age."

Children are great imitators. They must be taught by seeing, in action, what they are to believe and do.

P72 — "My people, I wish you could bring the children to Me in church, so they can be acquainted with My Word. By showing them example, the children will learn to visit Me at Church on Sunday and have respect for this day of the lord…. If the children see only what you say, and do not see it in your actions, then how do you expect them to follow My commands. Children are great imitators, and they will pick up all of your bad habits as well. Be watchful of your speech and your actions in front of your children.…"

Volume V — Oct to Dec '96

Parents' responsibility for passing on the faith. Parents' concern for the worldly — what about the spiritual?

P10 — "My people … It is your responsibility as parents to see that the faith gets passed on to future generations. Do not trust this responsibility to others to provide this training. You are the ones to reinforce the gospel message in your lives as an example to them. Guard their innocent souls from all evil influences around them."

P64 — "My people, many parents are very good at providing recreation and the proper schooling, but how many of these parents are as concerned with the spiritual lives of their children? It is even more important to teach them of the ways of faith than to have them brilliant in worldly knowledge. Many have still to learn that caring for their soul is the most important task that all parents need to take care of, since their souls are immortal. That which lasts forever is more deserving of your attention than all that is passing away before you."

Today's electronic marvels lead to the entrapment of children. Abuse by daycare providers and teachers

P95 — "My people, I love the children and I called them to Me at all times. Remember how I asked that no one should mislead the least of My little ones lest a millstone be placed around their necks and they be thrown into the sea. All of My children are precious and they need your protection from the evils of the world. Now, even your electronic marvels are attracting innocent children to entrapment by adults. You must watch your children closely, even from those whom you should be able to trust. **Daycare providers and even teachers are abusing My little ones.** Pray that their guardian angels may be attentive to their protection when they are out of your sight."

Volume VII — Apr to Jun '97

The need for moral values and to see the commandments being obeyed. The corruption of the movies.

P30 — "…Not only is it necessary for these children [those going to first Holy Communion] to learn the faith, it is also good for them to have moral values understood. They are beginning to know right from wrong, but they need to see the commandments being obeyed by their adult teachers. Sometimes the best way to teach children is by your good example. It is even more proper that the children be taught about the forgiveness of sin in confession, since they need proper preparation to receive me in My Eucharist. **They should know early on not to receive Me with mortal sin on their souls,** even as today's adults should remember. Help protect My little ones from harm and your reward will be great in Heaven."

P61 — "My people … the movies of your day have corrupted many souls. When your TV and theatres become an occasion for you, it may be best for your soul not to view such things. **The influence of these things on the children may harm these little ones of Mine in the formation of their consciences.** Guard yourself and the whole family from such temptations."

Volume VIII — Jul to Sep '97

Take the children to Mass. Those who refuse face judgement

P16 — "It is important that the children be taken to Mass to share in the knowledge of My love. Those parents who refuse to take their children to Mass will face a strong judgement in My eyes. The little ones seek Me and if you thwart this natural inclination, you will get more stripes than for not going alone.

"Grandparents and parents, watch over and protect the children. Put scapulars on them and give them rosaries."

P18 — "My people, many of My little ones are in an evil environment which could lead their souls away from Me. My dear parents and grandparents, I want you to watch over and protect your children from the evils of this world. Do not stand by passively and allow My little ones to be snatched by the powers of Hell ... be ... concerned for the spiritual lives of My children. Put on their scapulars and give them rosaries so they will have spiritual protection. Have faith in me by praying to watch over the children to protect them from evil."

Home teaching of the faith: a special grace. Day-care centres and schools

P41 — "My dear parents, remember you are responsible for bringing the knowledge of faith to your children and grandchildren. **For those that go to the trouble of teaching [the faith to] their children at home, a special grace will go out to your family.** In many places, the home may be the only place that your children may receive the proper training... be careful where you leave your children. Some children may be abused in various places of day-care. Even [at] accredited schools [they] may still receive the wrong influence from teachers who are not training with a proper moral code."

Parents' readiness to leave the children to others. Take a lesser standard of living. The deposit of faith

P46 — "My people, your children are pure and innocent at the outset. In your fast-paced society, you are too anxious to leave your children with others to be cared for. It is more important, where possible, to take a lesser standard of living so the mother can care for her young children. It is also important to know what your children are being taught. Give them each the deposit of faith that all of them need to come and know Me. It is your responsibility to lead their souls on the right path to Heaven...."

Children's prayers and worship on Sundays. Their spiritual welfare. Their spiritual mother and their Saviour

P69 — "Mary said: ... See that they learn their prayers and give honour and worship to My Son, Jesus, on Sundays. Love all of My children, as does My Son, and I want them to know His love as it is linked to my own. Help the children as much as possible to be exposed to Jesus' love in all they do. Jesus loves the little ones so much and He does not want to see any harm befall them. So be more open in looking out for the spiritual welfare of all children. This love of God needs to be instilled in all of my little lambs. So, **when you take them to school, remind them of their Spiritual Mother and their Saviour,** who are always watching over them."

Don't give up. Continue to pray for them. Remind them of Sunday Mass. They have to make their own decision

P73 — "My people, don't give up on your children at any age. Give them good spiritual direction by your example. It is your constancy in the faith and your persistence in winning their souls to Jesus that may be their salvation. Continue praying for them and gently reminding them of their duty at Sunday Mass. When you have done everything possible for them, you have done your part in being responsible for their souls. The children have to make their own decisions by their own free wills. Let the children come to Me out of love, by your direction."

Volume IX — Oct to Dec '97

Parents — spiritual guardians of the children. Show them God can help. Prayer at meals and bedtime. The rosary

P3 — "My people, you need to act as spiritual guardians for the souls of your children. Train them in good prayer habits and witness your prayer petitions to show them how God can help them. Pray at meals, at bedtime and any other time that you can say the rosary together. By your example, you can watch how your influence will guide your children on their path to Heaven. If your children should wander away, help them gently back to My fold. Never let them out of your spiritual sight."

Know what your children are being taught — even at college. The unknown evil influences

"My parents, it is your responsibility to see what your children are being taught. No matter what grade they are in, even college, ask them what is being taught. They could be getting evil influences that you would not know about. Sometimes your concern for their souls may alert them to the evil things going on in the schools. Teach them as well spiritually, as they receive education about worldly things. Your care must be constant and gently persistent in order to keep them from bad influences."

Encouragement by the demons of brainwashing of children. Test what they are being taught

P30 — "My people, beware of what the teachers are teaching the students both in secular classes and religious classes. The demons are encouraging evil teaching to brainwash the children against God. Test what your children and grandchildren are being taught. Do not leave the children in a spiritual vacuum. If they are not taught My love in prayer, they may be influenced by evil intentions."

Volume XIII — Oct to Dec '98

Children under the age of reason

P80 — "My people, I am reminding you … how My angels will be watching out for any evil spirit or evil person who will try to attack My little ones under the age of reason. Wherever they may be in the coming tribulation, I will protect their souls. Some may be martyred, but the rest I will care for in miraculous ways. Have this consolation that your young children will be cared for."

7. Suffering in Our Lives

"The redeemer suffered in place of man and for man. Every man has his own share in the Redemption. Each one is also called to share in that suffering through which the Redemption was accomplished. He is called to share in that suffering through which all human suffering has also been redeemed. In bringing about the Redemption through suffering, Christ has also raised human suffering to the level of the Redemption. Thus each man, in his suffering, can also become a sharer in the redemptive suffering of Christ." Apostolic Letter Salvifici Doloris *of the Supreme Pontiff John Paul II.*

"Those who share in the sufferings of Christ are also called, through their sufferings, to share in glory. Paul expresses this in various places. To the Romans he writes: "We are ... fellow heirs with Christ, provided we suffer with him in order that we may also be glorified with him." Apostolic letter Salvifici Doloris *of the Supreme Pontiff John Paul II.*

Volume III — Jul '95 to Jun '96

The crucifix to show Jesus' suffering body. In persecution — never lose hope in Jesus' love

P25 — "I tell you to return to My crucifix with My suffering body, so that you may well appreciate how much I suffered in My love for all mankind. I have died once for all men's sins, even for those to come. You My trusting servants, should also see in this, that if you are to be My disciple, you must also be willing to suffer for Me to gain your place in heaven. It is through suffering that you are humbled and tested to show your love for Me."

P34 — "Though you walk in the valley of darkness, either in this life or the next, you should fear no evil, for I am at your side to comfort you. No matter what persecution may lay in wait for you, never lose hope in My love. Each life is tested for its endurance and made stronger because of it. You will not avoid suffering in this life, but it behooves you to accept it gracefully, as you are free to give of yourself. Do not hold things back from Me, but be ready to give everything over to Me."

Jesus died for us: we must die to ourselves to obtain salvation. Jesus' suffering servants

P83 — "My people, think of the suffering I went through on the cross for love of you. If you see Me suffer, know that you will be asked to do likewise. I have died for your sins, but you must die to self, to obtain the blessing of salvation."

P142 — My people, many times you see those who are sick or infirm, and wonder why they are suffering. These are My suffering servants. Their pain is joined in My suffering on the cross, to atone for the sins of man. Therefore, be thankful for your health, but if you are suffering pain, offer it up as a prayer, so there will be more merits to help save sinners."

Jesus: still suffering for our ongoing sins. Offer all sufferings to the Father

P207 — "My people, you are seeing My suffering through My crown of thorns. I suffer much for your sins but, still, many do not realise I am still suffering for your ongoing sins, as well. I even suffer through My suffering servants on earth. There are many with severe sickness, which offer them up to Me for sin. Still other faithful ask to endure suffering to make up for sins of others.... However you suffer in this world, follow My example, and offer up your suffering to My Father as your prayer from the heart."

P211 — "...if you are to truly witness My death on the cross, you should promote this view on My true cross complete with the corpus. Those who do not show My suffering, cannot understand how they must suffer as I did, if they are to be saved."

Take up our cross daily and bear it lovingly for Jesus' Name's sake. Our purpose here is to suffer

P244 — "My people, I call on you every day to take up your cross and bear it lovingly for My Name's sake. Do not think you are put here to have only earthly enjoyment. Your purpose here is to suffer, as I have given an example so that you will purify your weakness to sin.... You have been given free will to choose to love Me or not. Pray, My children, that you may gain strength to fight temptations to sin. By yourselves you will fail, but with My grace, you will win your crown of salvation."

After confession: make reparation through prayer and fasting. Offer up all sufferings

P337 — "My children, after your confession, you should make an effort in prayer and fasting to make reparation for the punishment due for your sins. Your sins are forgiven, but My justice demands some payment either in suffering on earth, or in purgatory in the after life. Give up to Me all of your sufferings on earth to lessen your pain in the after life."

A Lesson From Jesus in carrying our cross

Volume III — 6 Jul '96

P345 — "My people, many times I have asked you to carry your cross, but I wish to give you even a better lesson.... My children, you must imitate Me in every way in life. Bear your cross of life as I did, with patience, even if you are insulted or persecuted. Do not fight back, but pray for your persecutors.

"As I fell carrying the heavy cross, do as I did, and pick yourself up whenever you are feeling down and depressed. Always carry on in faith, and I will see to your every need. When someone came to My aid, as Simon and Veronica, welcome people's help and be gracious to all of these generous souls. As My clothes were stripped from Me, I ask you to strip the worldly things from your life. As I had to suffer on the cross, you too, must suffer for My sake.

"Give all of your pain up to Me as a prayer, that I will store in heaven as payment for the reparation of your sins. As I was laid in the tomb, you too, are appointed to die, unless you are chosen for life in the tribulation. As I was resurrected, so you will experience your own resurrection. What I am showing you is that your life will follow in My footsteps, if you expect to be with Me in heaven. So, when I ask you to follow Me, this is the path I wish you to walk with Me. All those who wish to be saved must follow this path."

Understanding the Great Tribulation and the Era of Peace

Part III

An Alphabetical Reference to Some Messages Given to John Leary

"When love permeates everything you do, you experience my kingdom even on earth."
Message of 11 Nov '99

An Alphabetical Reference to Some Messages Given to John Leary by Our Divine Lord

Abortion: See also P98

Vol. VIII/68: 1 Sep '97 — "My people, this age is entering into **a spiritual darkness where life has no value**. Many millions of unborn children are condemned to death before they ever see the light of day. How long do you think I will allow this butchering to go on? … the killing goes on with only feeble attempts by some to stop this carnage.

"Even if you were to bribe these mothers to bring their babies to term for adoption, it would not change their hearts to holding life precious. In any way that is possible, people should be struggling to give the unborn the right to life. If this effort does not bring down abortion, then **My justice will rain down a destruction befitting your sins**. How many times have I told you, America, to wake up to your own holocaust and stop killing My babies?"

Vol. XV/17: 13 Apr '99 — "My people, once a baby is taken away, there is no more life, as in an abortion. Each life you snuff out is one more life never to be loved or shared with in growing up.

"You have seen in wars, how children were killed by ruthless soldiers. Again, the innocents killed by Herod were based on pride of keeping his throne. But abortions involve the child's mother killing her own baby out of 'convenience.' No reason and no price can be placed on a defenceless little one to be killed. The parents took the responsibility for this life when they conceived the child. It is not the child's fault if the parents did not want this child.

"I tell you that those who kill their children will have to anwer for it at their judgment.

"I will forgive even this grievous sin, if the parents come to Me with contrite hearts. Those who refuse to make amends for their crimes, will suffer much in the lowest places of hell, for I told you how it would be better for one who harmed My little ones to be thrown into the ocean with a millstone around their neck."

24 Nov '99 — "My people, many women, who find themselves with an unwanted pregnancy, feel like they are trapped in a corner. Some are quick to think of an abortion because of their embarrassment or the care and money of raising a child. *Remember that each baby is not really a part of your body and it is human from conception.* There is nothing you can value in place of another life. That is why killing a baby by abortion is equal to killing someone with a gun. You have the responsibility of conceiving the child as much as you have for taking care of this child.

"The doctors also are responsible for protecting life instead of taking money for abortions. This blood money of the doctors is the thirty pieces of silver they take for their acts of killing. I will see to it that this wealth will cause these doctors nothing but grief if they do not repent of their killings. These doctors and lawyers encourage the women to have so called 'safe' abortions, but they will pay for their crimes. Pray for these mothers, the doctors and your representatives that could remove these laws allowing abortions. Do everything you can to protect My babies or your country will pay for this blood on your hands. My cup is overflowing with your sins and My justice will be carried out in your chastisements."

Adoration:

Vol. III/311: 31 May '96 — "My people, I wish that you would all come to Me on your knees. **Kneeling** in humble adoration of My Blessed Sacrament **is your most proper posture** to give Me praise and adoration."

Vol. VIII/71: 4 Sep '97 — "My dear people, **when you come to Me in prayer,** it would help you to **kneel in adoration.** When you pray on your knees, you can be more disposed to Me and avoid distractions."

Angels:

Vol. II/55: 28 Aug '94 — "You are seeing [as in the vision] how I will separate the evil men from the faithful during the three days of darkness. **All My faithful will be marked with a cross on their foreheads,** while those evil men and women will be marked with the sign of the beast. I will send My angels to mark My faithful to be protected so that they will be passed over for purification much like the Hebrews were protected with the lamb's blood on their lintel. The devil and his angels will be allowed to take those unprotected souls. At that time, all unworthy souls and the demons will be sent to hell to purify the earth."

Vol. III/79: 2 Oct '95 — "My people, at your day of entering heaven, **your guardian angel will be escorting you to Me....** If you ask them they will help you in everything according to My Will."

Vol. III/256: 7 Apr '96 — "**...** It will soon come to a point, when evil spirits are loosed, that I will also loose the ability of My own angels to defend My faithful with their full force, without restrictions as now. **I will allow each soul freedom to choose Me or not,** such that the angels on either side will not be able to force your will...."

Vol. V/90: 26 Dec '96 — "My people, My angels are walking among you. As they place My mark on the foreheads of My faithful, **another angel records their name in My Book of Life.**"

Vol. XIV/86: 12 Mar '99 — "My people, **My angels have already marked those to be saved of My faithful.** Those who will convert after My warning have yet to be marked. That is why these souls, that you can evangelize, will have their last chance by My mercy."

Antichrist: See also P22.

Vol. I/19: 19 Sep '93 — "The Antichrist **will come from Egypt** (much like Jesus came out of Egypt). He will bring a false peace during an upheaval in the world. Prepare for the Antichrist — he will win many away from God."

Vol. I/36: 26 Oct '93 — A sign of the coming of the Antichrist to power will be a conjunction of stars. See below "Conjunction of stars."

Vol. II/30: 2 Aug '94 — "After this event [the warning] you will see the entrance of the Antichrist as he will come to power."

Vol. II/97: 14 Oct '97 — "You will see **many signs and wonders to announce the beginning of the reign of the Antichrist.** Know that **an eclipse** will usher in the evil days of darkness. At that time you should be in hiding to avoid the powers of darkness…"

Vol. III/23: 28 Jul '95 — "When he comes to power, he will rule the world through your purse strings. **As your Internet becomes more inclusive, you will see how he will send his messages over TV to all households with receivers.** He will mesmerise people with his eyes and his lies. His promise of peace to everyone will draw many to believe in him, but it will be lacking in love. By the time people realise his real intentions of power, it will be too late, since he will control their food and jobs."

Vol. III/46: 22 Aug '95 — "My people, **there will be no doubt in your mind when the time of the Antichrist will arrive.** His agents will readily trumpet his appearance. He will have charisma and the power of suggestion over many minds…. Many will want to elevate his position even to like a God in himself. Along with him will be an imposter pope who will try and mislead My Church."

Vol. V/55: 21 Nov '96 — "This will be the peak of Satan's reign in this man called the Antichrist. This **blue light in the sky is another sign of his coming** to earth in his public life. When you see the increased cold, this represents many souls' hearts will turn cold to as Me as well."

Vol. III/247: 29 Mar '96 — "The particulars of his identity are not necessary at this time. It is better not to seek this information, since he can use such information to control people.... **avoid him at all costs**..."

Vol. X1/49: 14 May '98 — "My people, there will be a great celebration in the Church before the coming of the Antichrist. **Many will be cheering Pope John Paul II for a while.** Then evil will prevail over Rome for a short time. It will be My triumph later that will usher in My renewed earth ..."

Vol. XV/35: 29 Apr '99 — "My people, **many will be protesting the atrocities of many injustices**. People will be frustrated with low-paying jobs and various shortages of your necessities. These problems will worsen at the end of the year and it may trigger the instability of many governments and financial systems. Be prepared **to endure major chaos right** before the Antichrist will take over."

24 Jul '99 — "...a secret government run by the people of money are behind the scenes controlling your lives... these people will assist the Antichrist to power as they will try to force the mark of the beast on everyone. **Do not be surprised when you see a manufactured crisis develop** and these monied people will openly take-over every government so the Antichrist can come to power."

25 Jun '99 — "My people, a time is coming when all of the governments of the world will crumble and fall into the hands of the Antichrist. Many do not want to believe that this can happen, but this is how it is written in the Bible.

"Once the Antichrist has assumed power, he will assign ten leaders as his puppets to help him control the whole world. He will set up a mark of his image to be worshiped and he will force everyone to buy and sell using his mark that will be placed in the right hand or forehead. The monied people of the new world order will control this new means of exchange through the central banks all over the world. There will be a network of satellites to control all of this buying and selling."

24 Nov '99 — "My people, **I have told you that everything is in place to bring control over your people**.

- You have several satellite systems that already are year two thousand compliant. These same satellites can be contacted by battery powered devices, and because the satellites use solar power, they will not be affected by power outages.
- You are seeing smart chips promoted for buying and selling and more Internet connections as well. All of these new systems will give the one world people more control over your lives in the next few years.
- National ID systems are being established in many countries to again bring your licenses and passports under the control of the one world people.

"All of these events, including your computer problems, are laying the foundation for control by the Antichrist. **Refuse to take the smart chips and absolutely refuse putting these chips in your body for any reason.** You would rather be martyred than be under the control of the Antichrist. Let Me provide for your needs and adore only Me. Have no fear as My triumph will soon come as the Antichrist comes to full power."

14 Dec '99 — "My people, as you look at this subway tunnel, this would be a good place to be during the early beginning of the tribulation. When you see wars, chaos and riots coming, these underground tunnels would afford you temporary protection. **As the reign of the Antichrist arrives, it would be then safer to be in the caves and refuges.** Toward the end of the Antichrist's reign, you will need to be on high ground far inland from the Eastern Seaboard [of the USA] to avoid being drowned by the large tidal waves. My people, prepare yourselves spiritually and physically, for the time of My triumph is near. Trust in My protection and I will guide you through the coming tribulation. Without My help, you will not be able to resist the evil ones' control. Do not take anything from the evil ones, but **rely solely on My miraculous help. Some will be martyred, but I will protect your souls from evil.**"

16 Dec '99 — "You would have to be deaf and blind not to understand that the age of the Antichrist will be coming in a very short time. Prepare your souls with confession and a repentant heart. You will have to call on My help to get you through this tribulation of persecution. Christians are being killed already in many countries. It is just a matter of time until you will see the martyrs' blood flowing in your own country. Already you have the blood of the little martyrs of abortion on your hands."

1 Jan 2000 — "Many of the plans of the Antichrist are taking shape in Europe and your multinational trade agreements. The controls of the one world people will gradually close a vice on your money through your stock markets and the control of your jobs. You are so taken up with your new found wealth, that you fail to see how vulnerable these markets are to control. As you see a movement toward a one world religion, you will see the beginnings of your open religious persecution. Call on My help in all of the trials you will face this year."

14 Jan 2000 — "My people, I have told you how the Antichrist would exploit all of your electrical devices to control people. More advertising and TV commercials are promoting smart cards and even a few ads promote the chip in the hand. The microwave signals being sent out from the skyscrapers in the vision will locate and control people in their smart cards and even more so in the chips in the body.

"These beams will send TV signals of the Antichrist to all the televisions in the area and you will see his face on the screen even if your set is not turned on. Those with chips and TVs will be influenced to worship the Antichrist and use his money and his food. I told you after the Warning to get rid of all of your TVs and computer monitors so you could not see this evil man's face."

Antichrist declaration:

Vol IX/61: 29 Nov '97 — Cables, telephones, TV, faxes, computers, copiers etc

"My people, I wish to warn you about the coming of the Antichrist and his declaration time. At the time of his first announcement about his coming in declaration, have all of your cables out of your house and do not watch your television any longer — disconnect them.

"**As it comes closer to the day of his declaration**, do away with your telephone lines, your computers, faxes, copiers, radios, and anything electronic that can be influenced by the demons, since they will use them to distract you. In addition to these, stop your newspaper and even your mail. All of these will be controlled."

Vol. VII/76: 18 Jun '97 — power in literature and pictures

"…as the time for Antichrist's declaration comes, he will gain in power and all literature or pictures about him will take on more power as well…. **do not have any of the Antichrist's writings or pictures around you.**"

Antipope: See also "Pope John Paul II"

Vol. VIX/88: 15 Mar '99 — "My people, your events are moving quickly to their completion. The time of a new 'pope' being installed is coming soon. It will be at this same time that **you will see My Pope son, John Paul II, being exiled**. Once this evil 'pope' takes over, he will quickly align himself with the world politics. He will establish new Church laws that will violate My old traditions. He will make a mockery out of My beliefs of the Faith. His ultimate insult to Me will be to encourage My faithful to believe in and worship the Antichrist. In search of his own power as a papal state, he will join a world alliance that serves the Antichrist.

"**Do *not* follow this evil 'pope,'** who will misguide people to sin. His false decrees are not supported by the Holy Spirit and their evil will be made known to My elect, so they will not follow these evil ways. Test this evil 'pope' by discernment and the fruit of his deeds. A bad tree cannot bring forth good fruit, nor can a good tree bear bad fruit."

April — a spectacular event:

28 Sep '99 — "My people, I have given you this number four to indicate the month of April. In this month in a given year you will see an event so spectacular, that the whole world will be influenced by it. Do not speculate on dates or try to assume what this event will be. As you get closer to significant events, I have been giving you enough information when you need it. This is another sign that you are drawing close to the time of tribulation. I am also stressing to my people to get their spiritual lives in order. If you knew that you were going to die tomorrow, would you do anything different today?"

Armageddon: See also P58

Vol. III/256: 7 Apr '96 — "You will see events gradually lead up to the final Battle of Armageddon, as then My victory will be proclaimed over sin and Satan. This conquest will be as astounding as the glory of My Resurrection."

Vol. VIII/91: 22 Sep '97 — "... an awesome battle ... will take place as the Antichrist seeks full reign of the world ... This final battle of good and evil at Armageddon will decide once and for all the almighty power that God has over creatures. It is God's Will that will be done ..."

18 Jan 2000 — "The battle of Armageddon looms in the Middle East and the battle lines are being drawn. It will be My triumph over these evil ones that will begin My new Era of Peace. Trust in Me that I will have My angels separate out the evil tares from the wheat of My flock. These evil ones will be chained in hell, while My faithful will have their reward in heaven and on earth."

Armed takeover:

Vol. VIII/87: 18 Sep '97 — "You will see armies suddenly take over your country, and they will imprison many in detention centres. Religious persecution will be rampant, and you will need to seek My refuges for safety. Pray, My children, to keep your sacramentals with you to fight this demonic attack."

Australia:

Vol. VIII/19: 17 Jul '97 — Mary said: "My dear children, thank you for your many rosaries tonight. Because of your prayers, I will raise up Australia before my Son as well. **People of Australia, listen to my requests.** By the power of your rosaries, you will hold up my mantle of protection against the evils of your land. If there is not enough prayer you will lessen my protection. So pray three rosaries each day and say my consecration prayers, so all of your souls may be close to my Son's heart. Seek His love, my children, and all else will be given to you."

Baptism:

8 Jan 2000 — "My people, baptism is an important sacrament because it initiates you into the people of God in My Church. When you are baptised as an infant, your godparents spoke for you in denouncing the devil and the world. As you grow and mature in your faith, there will come a time when you realise that you need My help to get you through life. It is this time of understanding when you will fully embrace Me as your Saviour. Once you give your life over to following My will, you can repeat your baptismal vows with meaning.

"The other calling of your baptism is to share your faith with others through evangelization. I asked My apostles to go out and preach My Gospel to all the nations. Parents can teach the faith to their children and any adult can be invited to accept Me in faith. Your invitation to Me may be the means of saving souls from going to hell. I even give a special mission to My messengers and prophets to bring My Gospel message to all who would listen to My Word and take it to heart.

"There is a joy in living your faith because it shows everyone that you truly believe and are not a hypocrite. Pray for poor sinners that they may see their errors and repent of their sins. Once they repent, they can be accepted into the faith through baptism."

Belief:

20 Jan 2000 — "My people, **many have refused to believe** that they are in the days right before the great tribulation of the Antichrist. I have witnessed to you the signs in your weather, your earthquakes, and the control of your computer chips in your buying and selling. I told you how when you see the trees budding and the weather warming, you know that spring is about to come. So, also, when you see the apostasy of your world, rampant sins against My commandments and signs in the skies, you will see the evil age of the Antichrist about to take over the world. Fear not, My people, for I will protect you against evil influences and I will provide for your needs. **Do not use these evil chips to buy and sell, but put your full trust in My protection.**"

St. Benedict cross:

Vol. III/275: 28 Apr '96 — "Remember how I have asked you to wear My crucifix with My corpus to be protection against the evil spirits. Your St. Benedict crosses, with a blessing, are indeed most proper for exorcisms. Give Me thanks for My great gift of spiritual life to all of you. Reverence Me, by having the crosses I desire in prominent places, as an example to my people."

Vol. VII/52: 27 May '97 — "… Have confident assurance that I will protect your souls from the onslaught attempts of the Antichrist…. You will need your Blessed Sacramental of your rosary and the St. Benedict Cross to ward off any evil you will face."

The Bible:

Vol. XIII/23: 17 Oct '98 — "My people, help Me to preserve My Church. I am calling on My faithful remnant to hold their faith close to their hearts. **Do not change your faith or listen to those who want to change My words in the Bible**. I have given you revelation of Myself in the Scriptures, so guard your current Bibles from any distortions."

Vol. XIV/3: 3 Jan '99 — "My people, you have seen the new Bible and Lectionary translations come out. There are some in different quarters that want My word translated **to fit their itching ears**. They are not satisfied with the way My inspired word was given, so they have changed it to fit their fancy."

Vol. XIV/148: 9 Feb '99 — "My people, you are taking too many liberties in the latest translation of My Scripture. **Today, you are appeasing the gender nature of the scriptures for a better hearing for certain women.** Even this reason is a little shallow, since the scripture writers wrote in a different culture from today. But (for) tomorrow you have set a precedent to appease other 'lifestyles', which are compromising the nature even of the sins of your times.

"The Scriptures **were not written to make everyone comfortable with the words**, they were written as revelation of My plan of your salvation. To that extent, My word cannot be compromised. Instead of encouraging many 'viewpoints' in your translations of My Bible, I would rather you kept the original translation. My laws are not changing with the ages. They are forever a light for you, to follow My road to heaven."

Bicycles:

Vol. III/47: 23 Aug '95 — "Have some bicycles ready to use when you need to leave for hiding. There may not be enough gas available at that time. Also you may encounter difficulties with running your car if the evil men wish to inactivate the electrical mechanisms inside the workings of your car."

Cables: see "Television"

California earthquake:

Vol. VII/29: 3 May '97 — "My people, this area will come under great devastation soon. You will see smaller earthquakes lead into a larger one of **8 magnitude**…. Many will be stripped of their possessions with some loss of life.... **This earthquake will be a major sign of the coming purification**, where evil will have its influence for a time."

Cameras:

23 Apr '99 — "My people, as your technology has improved, you are now being watched by security devices wherever you go. **Many of these chips can scan without usual cameras**, so you do not even know you are being watched. The one-world people want to know and control all of your movements. That is why your governments are using so many cameras and satellites to watch you. Soon your travel will be more restricted and it will be more difficult to travel over national borders. Even your expressways will soon require smart cards to travel them.

Cars: See also P35 — "The Need to Go into Hiding"

Vol. XII/28: 23 Jul '98 — I could see **an older vehicle over fifteen years old**. Jesus said: "My people, your older vehicles will be safer in bringing you to My safe havens. Newer vehicles will only be useful for part of your travel to your refuge destination. Do not fear or worry in how you will be protected. It is only your concern to remain faithful to Me and follow My will."

Vol. XIII/17: 12 Oct '98 — "... Lightning, solar storms and nuclear weapons have made all your microchips vulnerable to destruction. With a given frequency, microwaves can destroy your electronic ignition chips in your cars...."

Caves: See also P35 - "The Need to go into hiding"

Vol. XII/24: 21 Jul '98— "I am showing the caves deep in the earth where you will find hiding places from the Antichrist. There will be **springs of healing waters both for drinking and to heal your sickness**.... When you see the chariots burning, it is a symbol for you that My angels will keep you from harm. The evil men will not be able to reach you, no matter how sophisticated their devices are. My angels will wrap their arms of protection around you, so the evil demons will not be able to attack you...."

Vol. XII/86: 16 Sep '98 — "...I will provide a place of protection for you that will hide you from the evil men of that time. For some, My angels will lead you to caves in the hills. **By My miraculous help, the evil people will not be able to see you.** My angels will protect you from diseases and physical harm. At the same time I will provide food, water, and shelter."

Children: See also P104

Vol. II/68: 11 Sep '94 — Mary said: "...I, as your spiritual mother, am asking each parent and even grandparents to watch over these precious little ones. It is up to you to see that they receive a Christian upbringing so that they will be acquainted with My Son. In many cases you must direct them back to Church or pray for their conversions. **These are your charges, your responsibilities** since you helped bring them into the world. You are called to be apostles, but your own relatives should receive your first attention. My Son loves the children and wants them brought up in a loving Christian environment which you can provide."

Vol. VIII/73: 5 Sep '97 — "Do not give up on your children at any age. Give them good spiritual direction by your example. It is your constancy in the faith and your persistence in winning their souls to Jesus that may be their salvation. **Continue praying for them and gently reminding them of their duty at Sunday Mass.** When you do everything possible for them you have done your part in being responsible for their souls. The children have to make their own decisions by their own free wills. Let the children come to Me out of love, by your direction."

Vol. XIII/80: 3 Dec '98 — "My people, I am reminding you in this vision how My angels will be watching out for any evil spirit or evil person who will try to attack **My little ones under the age of reason.** Wherever they may be in the coming tribulation, I will protect their souls. Some may be martyred, but the rest I will care for in miraculous ways. Have consolation that your young children will be cared for."

Vol. XV/27: 22 Apr '99 — "My people, this latest trial of killings is a further example of the effects of your death culture on young adults. Many parents are not even aware of the effects of your evil **TV programming and virtual reality computer games** that are brainwashing your children with evil. Your computer networks are now providing ways for children to make bombs and secure weapons. Your permissive society of seeking instant gratification has raised your movies and programs to a violence level that makes this latest carnage into a reality. Seek to bring My love into your families before Satan destroys you.

"My people, your news reports daily killings, while your violent TV programming shows everyone how to kill. Is it any wonder that your children are imitating what they see? The real problem of your society starts with the evil influence of violent programs, even in your cartoons. **Why are you aghast at these latest killings when children can watch this everyday?** Wake up America, and get rid of your violent programs and movies. It would be better to turn off your TVs and stop going to movies until movie makers clean up their acts. Get rid of your drugs and pornography and your children will have a better environment for proper living.

"My people, as you are bent on spring cleaning, carry this over to your spiritual cleaning. Many of your children are lacking love because you do not give them enough loving attention. **Put aside all of your selfish interests and extra jobs, so your children can have a loving family environment.** When you have little contact with your children, you are breeding ways they will struggle to get your attention. Prayer in the family is also important to hold your family together in love. Without My presence among you, Satan will be causing more divorce and killings. Unless you can establish peace and love in your own families, you will not have peace in your world. Pray for each other that peace will be brought to families, nations, and the world."

China:

Vol. VIII/10: 8 Jul '97 — "… China will make its presence felt all over the world.… Any coming wars in Asia and Europe will be influenced by China."

Vol. XIII/26: 19 Oct '98 — "**They have designs on Taiwan, Korea and Japan.**… They are looking for help to build their war machine and gradually nationalise any foreign holdings in their country. This is a sleeping giant that still has communist world domination as its goal."

Comforts — of life:

30 Dec '99 — "My people, the glitter of worldly things are nothing but empty promises that will fade away with time. It is better to focus on Me and heavenly treasures that are everlasting. The human attraction for things of comfort as new cars and new homes, delights the mind initially. In your modern world of electronics you have many other appliances and computers to use up your time. The message I am giving you is **do not be taken up by any obsession to have the newest and expensive gadgets** that would totally occupy your time away from Me. These things are cold and devoid of love and some may not even work for long. I offer you a life of love both on earth and forever in heaven. Any comforts here are short lived and do not satisfy the soul.

"I offer you Myself in Holy Communion so your soul can be fulfilled in My love. A personal relationship with your God is far more important than anything you could find on earth. So do not be distracted by any earthly possessions that could take your love from Me. You see and experience physical things, but your soul seeks the perfection of a spiritual life with Me. Your love of your Creator has much more to offer than any passing thing on earth. So arrange your priorities in life to do everything to serve and love Me."

The Comet: See also P49 - "The tribulation"

Vol. VIII/45: 10 Aug '97 — "… **the comet of the great chastisement** … is already directed towards Earth and it will not be changed from its orbit. It will not be long before you will hear of its discovery. At first it will be kept secret so as not to raise fear among the people. The information will be leaked out as the military will try to destroy it. I have shown you before that My angels will deflect any attempts to destroy it.... This is the instrument that I will use to thwart Satan of his brief reign.

Vol. XII/59: 21 Aug '98 — "My people, I am showing you again the comet of My great chastisement that will be My triumph over Satan. **This comet is already on its way to your planet, but the scientists are not revealing it**. As it starts to approach you, many will see it and it will no longer be a secret. The missiles that will be sent to destroy it will not work as My angels will deter them. What is meant to happen will not be changed by mankind...."

24 Aug '99 — "Many of your scientists know of its coming, but they are keeping it a secret to prevent a panic. The only warning you will receive will come from amateur astronomers not sworn to secrecy. Even the news networks will not carry this story until it is about to hit the earth. Man will try to alter its path but what I have intended will not be destroyed."

8 Oct '99 — "My people, you will see a major celestial event when a part of a comet will affect the earth, but [it will not be] the final chastisement. Many will be frightened by this event, but **it will coincide with My warning experience**. As you all see your sins and how I would judge you, some may be frightened also to see their judgment in how you offended Me." (See also "Warning" below)

Computers:

Vol. XV/83: 10 Jun '99 — "My people, your technology has advanced so fast, that you have not planned for any failures in your equipment. You have been content to replace older computer chips with more powerful ones, but the built in flaws in your hardware and software have been intentionally overlooked. Those in control of your society have known about your date problems, but they have not planned enough to fix it on purpose.

"This is the means by which the Antichrist will be given his chance to rebuild a controlled people. Pray to me and your angels to lead you to safe places away from the evil plotting of men."

Vol. XV/92: 17 Jun '99 — "…your computers will not be working much longer. Man has been so proud of his accomplishments, but now **all of your society will come crashing down** with the year two thousand problem. Many have proposed ways to fix this problem, but your leaders would have none of it. You are dealing with a planned destruction of modern life as you know it.

"**Prepare to face a very mundane lifestyle in your next year**. The one world people are planning your demise. They will then bring forth the mark of the beast to control the people. Do not be influenced by evil's solutions. Depend on what I have asked you to prepare and with My help you will succeed in saving your souls."

3 Aug '99 — "You have been hearing every power plant, most banks and even governments saying they are year 2000 compliant to set the people's minds at rest. The real problem is that they are not telling you the truth and they really are not sure if their fixes will work. They do not want to cause panic now, but they are only postponing the problem until later. Many nuclear plants and coal plants are not compliant and it only takes a few to go offline to cause a breakdown on your grids. Without power many of your conveniences will not work. That is why I have been telling you to prepare for the worst with food, water, and fuel in colder areas."

27 Oct '99 — "My people, you have prided yourselves on your computer advances, but you failed to fix an obvious problem.

"By errors in your management and planned malfunctions, your computer age is about to crash with many repercussions on your way of life. The domino failures in your power, water, and banking needs will cause many people to panic into a chaotic situation.

"You will see some major financial setbacks that could cause a world depression. The degree of problems will be controlled by how each person adjusts to their needs. Pray, My people, and be prepared spiritually and physically for the trials you are about to face. The one world people will exploit this crisis and they will allow the Antichrist to come to power. **A new compliant computer system will evolve that the evil people will use to control people with chips in the hand.** Refuse this mark of the beast wherever you are and focus on My help at My refuges. Those who stay faithful to Me will enjoy eternal life with Me."

25 Dec '99 — "My people, you have just celebrated all of the gift giving at Christmas and you are still contemplating My coming at Bethlehem. Just as it seems only a few short years after My birth that I had to suffer on the cross, even now in a few days you will have to consider your computer problems in the new year. You may have to suffer some shortages of power because that is the darkness of the vision. Along with power outages, you will have problems heating your houses in certain areas.

"**That is why you are seeing the fireplace for those who can heat with wood that are prepared.** I have asked you to store food, water and fuel because of the coming world famine, the computer chips in the body, and your computer problems next year. **Those who do not heed My messages may be cold and hungry for a time. Remember that following your faith and keeping My sacramentals around you will help you fend off any evil influence.**"

Computer monitors:

14 Jan 2000 — "These beams [as in the vision] will send TV signals of the Antichrist to all the televisions in the area and you will see his face on the screen **even if your set is not turned on.** Those with chips and TVs will be influenced to worship the Antichrist and use his money and his food. I told you after the warning to **get rid of all of your TVs and computer monitors** so you could not see this evil man's face."

Communism:

Vol. III/234: 15 Mar '96 — "My people, you have grown used to the idea that communism is dead. I tell you it will raise its ugly face once again.… **Russia** may soon lapse back into their old familiar ways of atheism. **China has remained a sleeping giant**, ready to flex its muscles, whenever it seems time for their move. I have warned you many times to not cease praying for peace in your world."

Confession: See also P75

25 Jan 2000 — "My people, I am showing you how important it is to have your sins washed away in the graces of confession. Just as you bathe each day to take away the dirt off of your body, so your soul needs to be scrubbed of its mortal sins in the spiritual bathtub of confession. By coming to the priest, he will absolve you of your sins and he takes My place on earth. **It is not very hard to physically drive or walk to the church for confession.**

"You may have to swallow your pride that you are a sinner, but do not fear the priest. I am waiting for you, so I can release you from the bondage of your sins. I give you free will to love Me or not, but those who refuse Me and fail to wash away their sins in confession will have to suffer the punishment for their sins. **Better to make your amends here in this life than suffer eternity in the flames of hell.** I am merciful and loving, but I am just as well. Come to the cleansing waters of My sacraments, especially confession, and you will be spiritually clean and ready to be received into heaven. Repent now while you still have time."

26 Jan 2000 — "My people, I am showing you this dirty window as a look into your soul. The more you sin, the dirtier the window becomes, until it is very hard to keep your focus on Me. This is why seeking My forgiveness of your daily sins is ever so important. **For your serious or mortal sins it is necessary for My faithful to cleanse your souls in the graces of confession.** In your cars you turn on windshield wipers so you can see clearly. It is the same with your souls. It is important to constantly clear away the distractions of the world and your sins through My forgiveness.

"I give this message often and in many ways so you can remember this lesson to keep a clear focus on My love through prayer and fasting. Working to keep your faith takes a lot of maintenance and renewal. No matter how much your soul becomes weighed down in sin, I am always at your side to take them away with your contrite heart and your desire to be forgiven. **You are seeking to be with Me in paradise, but you must work hard toward your perfection, even despite your weaknesses.** Then when I come for you, you will have your rest with no further evil temptations."

Confusion — about events:

3 Jan 2000 — "My people, many of the Jews remarked to Me how I taught with authority and even some questioned by what authority did I speak. I answered their questions with a question of St. John the Baptist's baptism of whether it was from God or man. This threw them into confusion and they no longer pursued the matter. So it is now that some may be in confusion about events and their timing. I have graced you with a time of mercy before the more serious events are to take place. There is no reason to despair over not being tested with more problems that have not taken place. **I am in control of events at all times, and you need to be focused on My will for each person.**"

Conjunction of stars:

Vol. I/36: 26 Oct '93 — "There will be a conjunction of stars, as at the Star of Bethlehem. Only this time it will be **a sign of the coming of the Antichrist coming to power**. It will be visible to those on the ground and the astronomers will witness it to the people. From that moment, the demons will be loosed to roam the earth and they will trouble men's souls."

Vol. II/171: 5 Jan '95 — "I have told you previously that a sign in the heavens, **like a star**, will announce the coming of the Antichrist much as I was announced at Bethlehem. But know that it will not be through any power of the evil one that this will happen. I will do this through My power as a sign to you."

Consecration:

Vol. VIII/72: 5 Sep '97— "Your current places of worship will soon become corrupt in their practices. When the priests change the proper consecration, My real presence will no longer be there."

Vol. XII/86: 17 Sep '98 — "Those who kneel during the consecration and receive My Host on the tongue are like this woman [as in the day's Gospel] giving Me heartfelt reverence. If you really recognised your loving God is present on the consecrated Host, you would kneel and bow in homage. When I come again, all mankind will bow in homage. Give honour and praise to Me before My Tabernacles and at perpetual adoration."

5 May '99 — "My people, I give you a quotation from Philippians 2:9-10. 'Therefore God also has exalted him and has bestowed upon him the name that is above every name, so that at the name of Jesus every knee should bend of those in Heaven, on Earth, and under the Earth.' This is the reverence I seek from you at the sound of My name. **I ask you also to kneel before My real presence at the consecration of the Mass.** When you pass by My Eucharist in the tabernacle, **I ask you to genuflect** in giving Me praise and adoration."

Creation:

Vol. IX/5: 4 Oct '97 — "My people, I am showing you about your origins from the first man. Many of your theologians have taken liberties in their interpretation of Genesis. I have told you before that the creation account is the belief that I have revealed to you. **This vision of humanity descended from one man is true and it is not meant to be debated....** All that was described has come to pass and all that is foretold will come to pass."

Cross: See also "luminous white crosses"

Vol. I/30: 16 Oct '93 — "There will be **a miracle of a permanent sign with the cross in the sky**. It will be visible to all and it will be a supernatural event to witness God's presence on earth. Those of faith will praise it and thank God for this precious visitation. Others will refuse to believe in it and will hide their faces from it."

Vol. II/55: 28 Aug '94 — "... You are seeing [as in the vision] how I will separate the evil men from the faithful during the three days of darkness. **All My faithful will be marked with a cross on their**

foreheads, while those evil men and women will be marked with the sign of the beast. I will send My angels to mark My faithful to be protected so that they will be passed over for purification much like the Hebrews were protected with the lamb's blood on their lintel. The devil and his angels will be allowed to take those unprotected souls. At that time, all unworthy souls and the demons will be sent to hell to purify the earth…"

Vol. V/90: 26 Dec '96 — "My people, My angels are walking among you. As they place My mark on the foreheads of My faithful, **another angel records their name in My Book of Life.…**"

Vol. XIV/86: 12 Mar '99 — "My people, **My angels have already marked those to be saved of My faithful.** Those who will convert after My warning have yet to be marked. That is why these souls, that you can evangelize, will have their last chance by My mercy."

Vol. VIII/58: 21 Aug '97 — "My people, be careful to test all the miraculous signs that will be given to you. Satan will try to imitate My crosses in having them strangely appear. Test the fruits of the spirit at these places. Trust more in crucifixes that have My corpus on them. The evil one cannot witness to My suffering on the cross. **When you hold up My crucifix, it will reveal to you if a miracle is from Me or Satan.**"

30 Aug '99 — "My people, as you see the light focused on My cross, it is My suffering that I want you to remember more than My Resurrection. **It is the cross that each of you must carry in life.** If you refuse to carry it with Me and for Me, you will find a heavier cross of frustration and despair. It is not easy to face your cross every day, but when you are focused on Me, your burden will be light."

Darkness — three days of:

Vol. II/55: 28 Aug '94 — "You are seeing [as in the vision] how I will separate the evil men from the faithful during the three days of darkness. All My faithful will be marked with a cross on their foreheads, while those evil men and women will be marked with the sign of the beast. **I will send My angels to mark My faithful to be protected** [see "Cross" above] so that they will be passed over for purification much like the Hebrews were protected with the lamb's blood on their lintel. The devil and his angels will be allowed to take those unprotected souls. At that time, all unworthy souls and the demons will be sent to hell to purify the earth…"

Vol. IX/35: 5 Nov '97 — "My people, what I am showing you is the beginning of **the three days of darkness.** After the comet strikes, there will be a massive volcanic activity. You will see the fire of the volcanoes on the horizon. As much dust and ash will be released into the air, then the sun will be completely blotted out. It is at that time that you need to be inside and not looking out at the lost souls who will be burning in a living hell on earth.

"**Only blessed candles will give light at that time.** Have faith that I will protect My faithful during this cataclysm. After the plagues of revelation are over, I will chain Satan, his demons and all the evil people in hell. Then the renewal of the earth will take place, and I will bring My faithful back to a renewed earth as the Era of Peace will begin. Rejoice, My people, for those living at this time will enjoy paradise on earth as Adam experienced."

Demons:

10 Nov '99 — "My people, you need to be strong to fend off temptations and focused on Me to keep your faith. The evil demons are ugly in their appearance if you saw them. **They are like ravenous wolves trying to tear souls apart.** They play on your pride, your laziness, and many worldly distractions to take your mind off of Me.

"By keeping you away from Mass and My sacraments, they can wear you down in your sins. **By going to confession, Holy Communion and having a good prayer life, you can fight off all of the evil one's temptations.** Be spiritually alert at all times, so with My help, you can fight off the trials of the devil's suggestions. By prayer and relying on My strength, I will lead you on your path to heaven."

Depression: See also P7 - "The famine"

Vol. VIII/61: 24 Aug '97 — "…As the famine and pestilence comes to the world, many will be fighting for goods and food. **There will be a massive world depression** that will cause national economic systems to falter and some will fail. Many will become so desperate for help to quell the riots and food shortages, that they will accept the man of peace in the Antichrist.…"

Vol. XIII/18: 13 Oct '98 — "My people, many are optimistic that your world scene will get better. I tell you to prepare for hard times because **a contrived world famine and a world depression** are on the horizon.…"

Detention centres:

Vol. VIII/12: 10 Jul '97 — "My people, you have been advised that many detention centres are being set up all over your country [ie USA]. These are places connected with the UN occupational forces throughout your country. Truly, now the one world forces are even moving their operations into your national parks. All of this should be of no surprise, since I told you Satan's agents are preparing for the coming of the Antichrist. Fear not, My people, as evil will be great, My power over evil will be greater. Your protection from the demons will be carried out by My angels."

Discernment: See also P27 - "False prophets"

Vol. III/124: 20 Nov '95 — Some people will receive the gift of discernment so they will be able to see in a vision **flames about those who are lost** and who will be a threat.

Disease: See also P49 - "The tribulation — comets, earthquakes, volcanoes, disease, weather control."

Vol. VIII/84: 16 Sep '97 — "My people, beware of the coming diseases and pestilence that will be coming in the last days. You will see new vaccine resistant strains of germs that will again cause huge epidemics…. Your manipulation of genes in medicines and plants will be another cause for concern. **Those gifted with healing will be sought out**. See, those who defy My love will have to suffer many plagues here as their punishment at the end of this age. As many will die from these outbreaks, there will be much chaos and terror for those who survive. Be faithful to Me in adoration and in your prayers, and I will protect you from these new germs…"

Vol. XII/70: 1 Sep '98 — "…As the time of the tribulation draws near, these evil men [in the military] **will be spreading disease germs in rural areas** where they suspect My faithful of hiding. You will be protected by My angels at all of My safe havens and the caves from any sickness. Look on the luminous white crosses or drink the healing waters at the caves and you will be healed of any plagues or diseases."

Vol. X/79: 12 Mar '98— "You will see a pestilence of disease grow across your nation and other nations. Many will die before cures will be found. There will be little defense from these sicknesses, as they will die out as quickly as they came."

Disaster:

19 Aug '99 — "… **Soon you will see one storm or disaster after the other**. If you will not pray on your knees, you will be humbled in the loss of your possessions. As your disasters reach to all corners of your country, you will then fall on your knees asking for My mercy. Pray for your country and your world which grows more evil each day."

19 Aug '99 — In Turkey. "… this is nothing compared to the **future earthquakes that you will see in your country.** Large earthquakes will be testing your country soon in several locations. Prepare your souls now to have your souls ready for judgement… you have a forewarning of what your own disasters will cause. As your storms and computer problems combine, you will see more flames of destruction throughout your whole country. **Be prepared to suffer destruction that you have yet to see on a scale you can-**

not even comprehend. Your country will be devastated and everyone will be shaken out of their complacency into a desperate people
calling on My help…"

6 Jan 2000 — "My people, I have told you that you would continue to see natural disasters occurring one right after the other.
You have just witnessed more destructive tornadoes and even some
problems in your computers. Even in other countries as in Brazil
and Europe, you have seen violent wind and floods. Many of these
disasters in nature are a result of the sin in your world.

"My people, earthquakes and other natural disasters will continue to give evidence of your end times. The eyeglasses on the
ground [as in the vision] symbolise that **even your most learned
people refuse to believe** that they are in the end times."

Dress:

Vol. XI/101: 27 Jun '98 — "My people, you are not animals, but
spirit and body. So **come appropriately dressed when you enter
my house.** Give Me honour and respect in your dress no matter
how hot your weather is. When you come to a wedding, you dress
to give respect to your hosts. When you come before your God,
should I not receive even more respect? Do not dress immodestly,
lest you cause someone to lust in looking on you. Be careful in
everything you do, that it be proper to please Me by your actions."

DNA manipulation: see gene manipulation

Earth orbit:

Vol. IV/11: 23 Jul '96 — "… you will continue to see volcanic
eruptions increase, but this one [as in the vision] will occur as the
comet strikes the earth. There will be a **tremendous distortion of
the earth's crust** which will give rise to many such volcanoes. It
will be a combination of these eruptions and the comet's own debris
that will give rise to the three days darkness. Other repercussions
will be a **changing of the magnetic poles** from their present position, and also a brief change in the earth's orbit away from the sun.

"**The gravity of the sun will correct this change in orbit**, but for a while the earth will be colder. It is during these three days of darkness that a cave or underground dwelling will afford you the best protection from the **cold and the sulphur in the air** depleting the oxygen for a short duration. Pray, My people, and listen to My instructions, and I will direct you where to go and how I will feed you with My Heavenly Bread."

Earthquake: See also "California"

Vol. XI/52: 16 May '98 — "My people, you will begin to witness an increase in earthquakes as a result of an increased solar wind from the sun. **Massive eruptions on the sun** will be affecting your communications and brownouts will occur with this increased solar activity. Many signs will be happening soon in your skies to give further witness of the coming end times…. Once these things are put into motion, **many will be shocked into panic,** because they did not believe in My prophesies. Your time is short before the tribulation will be upon you. Believe and prepare for this evil that will reach a height that you could not believe possible. With prayer and a request for My help, you will be protected from evil in many miraculous ways."

End times:

Vol. III/22: 27 Jul '95 — "My people, I have given many signs in the weather, in happenings and in messages, and still there are those who do not recognise these times as foretold in the scriptures. For those who do not understand My calling, or those who refuse My help, pray dearly that their hearts may be softened and more open to My love… Pray much for conversion."

6 Jul '99 — "… it is not for you to know the exact dates for when the end times will be brought about. **You will be given signs in the sky when they are near.** Do not worry about a particular date, but only put your faith in My words of My coming triumph. I will bring these things about in My way and in My time. Continue to serve Me in love and love your neighbour as yourselves. This is enough for you to follow until these events take place. **For if predicted dates do not happen, you will not lose your faith in Me.** Today has enough troubles of its own, so do not concern yourself with worries of tomorrow. I know it is human to be curious of such predictions, but live the moment of today, and do not spend your time thinking so much of the events of tomorrow."

4 Aug '99 — "… many are starting to understand that the signs of the end times are all around them. Some want to deny that the weather is unusual, but the facts and events tell the true story. Your signs of the end times will become more apparent with the events of this year. Your computer problems and military control may be coming to a head soon…"

14 Aug '99 — "… My angels are about to announce **the scrolls, trumpets and plagues of the end times.** Those who love Me and follow My will are to be protected from the evil ones and you will see the glory of the places I have prepared for you. Everyone is given free will to choose to love Me or reject Me. I do not force anyone to love Me. In the end though there will only be two places a soul can go. You will either be wrapped in ecstasy adoring Me for eternity in heaven or you will be in the torments of hell being hated forever by Satan and the demons. Many of the trumpets and plagues are the suffering that those who reject Me must suffer on earth before their eternal suffering in hell."

23 Nov '99 — "My people, I have not given you the date of My second coming, but **I have given you the signs of the end times to discern for yourselves.** Some may say that you have had similar signs before, but what I have given you is that:

- everything is in place to bring about the time of the Antichrist;
- You are witnessing the increase in earthquakes, the pestilence in diseases, and the signs for a world famine;
- You have the mark of the beast ready to be forced on everyone with a chip in your body for those who trust in man."

Era of peace: See also P64

Vol. I/151: 27 Mar '94 — "...There will be an era of peace ushered in at My Mother's triumph. But there will be a fierce battle of good and evil before that time. You must prepare, as I have warned you before, for this battle… Stay close to Me in prayer and the sacraments."

Vol. V — See also "Glorified bodies"

Vol. VI/84: 27 Mar '97 — "… The leaders of My Church have made **binding interpretations of 'Millenarianism'** which I wish to acknowledge under obedience to My Magisterium. They have not interpreted one thousand years to be taken literally. I will not then reign in My body. Only spiritually will I be present…. Suffice it to say now, when the time comes, you will experience the truth as I have willed it." (See also Catechism of the Catholic Church — No. 676)

26 Nov '99 — "My people, in the description of the end times in My Scriptures it speaks of My triumph over the beasts. I will come on the clouds to judge the people of this age, and the evil people and evil spirits will be dispatched to hell. I will then recreate the earth and I will bring down My new Jerusalem and there will reign an Era of Peace on earth. The vision I have given you (Isaiah 40:3) is how I will smooth the mountains, fill in the valleys, and straighten the crooked roads.

"The earth will have much vegetation and there will be beautiful weather. **There will be no evil on the earth and My people will praise Me in your growing perfection.** My kingdom on earth will reign in splendour and all will know of My power and love. Rejoice, My people, when you will live in this era for those who are faithful to My ways."

Evangelization:

Vol. VII/12: 14 Apr '97 — "All of you who have been baptised have that … calling to go out and bring souls to Me in the faith. All those who evangelize in My name will receive a prophet's reward. The harvest of souls is ready before this tribulation."

Vol. VIII/19: 17 Jul '97 — "My dear people, if you would be great in Heaven, you must serve the rest. My souls in the world are being attacked by Satan and his demons. I am asking all My faithful to serve in evangelizing the lost souls. Many souls do not realise the danger their souls are in because your society has grown more evil over time. These messages are being sent as a wake-up call to those souls far from Me. My children, invite these souls to My love and encourage them with your good example."

25 Jan 2000 — "When you are each called to evangelise, think that you are planting seeds of faith that require constant nurturing as when you grow grass. Coming to Me in faith is the first step and many need this personal invitation to move them forward to at least consider the possibility of converting. After this first step, a new convert must develop a personal relationship with Me as a deep commitment. Encouraging others in their prayer lives, as well as teaching them about the faith, are your ways to bring souls to Me.

"**Call on My help in My sacraments to further enhance the faith of new converts**. Many times you are also called to encourage even fallen away Catholics to return to their roots. You must deal with those who are spiritually lazy and find ways through My help to inspire their faith with a desire to love Me and their neighbour. It is this flame of love that must be ignited in every soul if they are ever to see My light."

Evolution:

Vol. VII/69: 12 Jun '97 — "My people, many of your scientists talk of your evolution from monkeys. **Man was created as I have shown you in the scriptures.** Man is the only species made to My image with a soul directed to Me. You are specially made and very different from other animals. Many decisions in your courts have perverted the truth."

Faith:

7 Jan 2000 — "Without My help you would not be saved in this coming time. That is why it is necessary now for you to build up your faith in Me by improving your prayer life. You will have to trust in Me completely in order to have your soul protected in this trial. Have no fear of these evil spirits. They may taunt you and threaten the body, but I will protect your souls. **You will suffer a living purgatory on earth**, but it will prepare you for the time of My triumph when I will bring you into My Era of Peace as a reward for your faithfulness."

20 Jan 2000 — "My people, I am asking you to proclaim your faith from the rooftops. You are My witnesses to My life, death and resurrection. Many have not seen Me, but My apostles passed on My words in My Gospels. **Do not be afraid to proclaim My word, no matter how much you may be persecuted.** Better for you to obey Me than obey man. You are My instruments so the sinners and the lukewarm will hear your words of invitation and take it to heart."

20 Jan 2000 — "My people, you will have to be strong in your faith to refuse worshiping any other god but Me. I am your Creator and the only One worthy of your worship. Refuse to take anything from the Antichrist whether it be food or jobs. Do not believe any of his lies and only believe in My coming victory. These evil ones will have a short reign before they will suffer a living hell on earth and an eternal suffering in hell itself. Call out to all sinners to give them one last chance to repent. If they fail to heed your words of My love and My commandments, then they will be judged by their own deeds."

False theologians:

Vol. XII/62: 25 Aug '98 — "My people, I am preparing you for the coming schism in the Church that will split My Church in two. My remnant will have their Masses underground in their houses. In addition to Mass needs, it will be necessary that you are well versed in your faith. Many false theologians will come forward saying how great the antipope is. By knowing the faith given by the apostles, you will be able to refute new heresies and blasphemies that will be used to mislead My faithful.

"You will be given the grace and the courage to break away from this new false church that will claim its roots in me. As true doctrine will be denied and new false dogmas will be proclaimed, people will be forced to choose between My remnant and the Antipope. **This is why you will need your old Bibles and your catechisms** to show the tenets of My true faith and the deceptions of the evil ones. By standing firm in your beliefs, you will save your souls."

Families:

20 Aug '99 — "When your families are so torn by divorce and a disrespect for marriage, it is no wonder that your nation is falling apart from within. Your disrespect for life follows from the evil that has destroyed the morality that used to be taught in the home. Your country has a great legacy in your founding documents, but now your laws support killing even the infants in the womb. Your court system is in disarray as much as your families. Pray, My people, that your leaders change the course of your laws, or more innocent people will die at their hands."

Famine: See also P7

Vol. XII/80: 10 Sep '98 — "My people, you have abused your land for other purposes than growing crops. Because you have despoiled the land in your waste, much of your land will turn into deserts and dust bowls. This will be the beginning of you world famine. All of these consequences are coming from your own hands. Pray for My help in providing for your needs. I will multiply food and water for those who trust in My miracles."

Vol. XIII/18: 13 Oct '98 — "...I tell you prepare for hard times because a contrived world famine and a world depression are on the horizon. The one world people need to create a crisis in order to cause the chaos that will enable their takeover. When enough are in fear, the Antichrist will come as a man of peace to solve all your problems…"

8 Jul '99 — "…There will be **a world famine** that will be brought about by poor growing conditions and by the manipulation of evil men in authority. **It will be the method of distribution of your food in this famine that will create many shortages.** The powers in authority will force people to take the mark of the beast and worship his image before he will allow them to buy food.

"This famine, wars, and your computer problems will all coincide to present a crisis that the Antichrist will use for his takeover."

23 Dec '99 — "My people, the few cattle that I am showing you are a sign of the coming famine. Some farmers are being tested by droughts, floods, and natural disasters so their feed crops have dwindled and they have had to cut down their herds. Since they have little feed and have to deal with increased disease, the animal herds are becoming low in numbers. There are more people filling the earth, but food resources are not keeping pace as more farmland has gone to develop housing.

"You are seeing **the signs of a coming famine** in your food shortages and distribution problems. Your weather patterns are changing that are not compatible for growing crops. I have told you to **store one year's supply of food and water** for this coming world famine and the restrictions of those trying to place the mark of the beast on many. By your faith in My multiplying your food, you will be watched over and provided for without fear. Listen to My words of preparation for your tribulation and you will be grateful for My help."

Fasting and self-control:

Vol. VIII/42: 7 Aug '97 — "You have many comforts and fine foods. Do not become so influenced that you appease all your appetites in an unbridled manner. Protect your body from excesses and train your self-control with fasting. Be willing to suffer for

My name's sake all that you are tested with. See with My help that your trials will seem easy to suffer as a prayer to Me."

Fires:

7 Oct '99 — "My people, **as you read in Revelation, there will be great fires all over the earth as a plague.** You are seeing fires in dry areas, in many disastrous accidents and in several volcanoes. This is another scourge of mankind that you are suffering as **a chastisement for your sins.** It is also a foretaste for those who refuse to accept Me into their lives. The evil ones will taste of many flames eternally in hell. Pray for conversions to lessen the number of souls being lost in hell."

Food: See also P7 - "The famine"

12 Aug '99: Control via prices — "… your chastisements of droughts, fires and storms are continuing unabated. Certain quarters are controlling the food prices to keep them artificially low so they can bankrupt the smaller farmers… The agents of Antichrist will use jobs and food to control the crowds to prepare for world takeover."

17 Nov '99: For the coming trial — "My people, I am showing you this picnic scene to indicate how to prepare for your coming trial. **Foods that you would take to a picnic** will be the best to adapt to little fuel and very little heating. To live in your home you will need food and water. As things progress to more serious problems both from your computer problems and manipulations of your leaders, you will eventually see martial law declared. It is with this declaration that many Christian groups will be threatened for not going along with the one world people."

1 Jan 2000: Storage — "You should keep your focus on the control of your jobs, the use of smart cards and smart chips in the body, and the status of activities in My Church in Rome. **The food and water you were asked to prepare was not just for the beginning of 2000, but for a world famine where food will**

be short, and when you do not have the mark of the beast to buy and sell."

Focus:

9 Dec '99 — "My people, many people's love of God is based on deep traditions that hold their lives together through what they believe. It is important that you know and practice your faith with real fervour. I should be the focus of your life and not just the one hour you set aside each week. Prayer and fasting is necessary if you are to build and sustain your faith. Guard your faith as a precious jewel, because if you lose it, your life would have no purpose. Do everything to encourage your family members to pass on the traditions of your faith. Once you water down your beliefs, your society will crumble from within. **Pray to hold your hearts close to Me and I will wrap My arms of protection around you."**

"My people of America, you are caught up in an age of technology which honours and even worships man for his own inventions. Do not get so distracted by your devices that you lose sight of your dependence on Me. As much as you want to be independent, you are very much dependent on My love and My creations. **Be satisfied with a simpler and slower paced life** which is better for your souls. Never lose your focus on serving Me, because if you serve the devil's ways, you could lose your eternal life. You will soon see how your technology will fall flat on its face in dismal failure. Whenever you depend only on yourselves, you will face destruction. Depend on Me in everything you do and I will reward My faithful in heaven."

7 Jan 2000 — **"Your goal is to know, love and serve me.** You cannot love me and money at the same time. Do not let this fast paced society control you by its greed for money. You do your work in a fair manner, but your off time is under your control and that is your time to focus on prayer and the real destination of your life. Do not let your jobs so possess you that you spend so much of your off time preparing for the next day. Your employers are invading your private time for their own gain. Getting ahead in your job is not worth ruining your health and forgetting about time for Me.

Your life passes by fast enough without increasing your pace of living.

"You need time to meditate on My laws and assess your growth in faith. You cannot think of Me if you are spending most of your time running after more money than you really need. You need to be focused more on depending on Me for help than relying on your massed up wealth. I am your God and not your money. **Focus on your eternal destination more and you will see the futility in chasing after money.**"

Gene manipulation:

Vol. XV/17: 27 Apr '99 — "My people, in your quest for knowledge, your scientists have discovered the workings of the genes in a cell's DNA. But man was not satisfied with knowing how life works. Now you are trying to improve on My plans of creation. All of your efforts to improve a plant or a person's DNA will end in ultimate failure, because you lack the total understanding of My plan for life. Man is always trying to exploit nature for profit, but you ultimately end up losing your goal. **Your failures in creating antibiotics that will kill all diseases have created monster mutants of diseases with no cures.**"

Germ warfare: See also "Disease"

Vol. XI/17: 14 Apr '98 — "There will come upon you **an airborne disease of suspicious origin**. It will have the symptoms of a severe case of pneumonia, only the doctors will have difficulty in developing a cure. This will come from a planned germ warfare to cut down on the population. As the time of the tribulation comes, you will find a healing for many of the coming plagues at My places of refuge...."

Glorified bodies:

Vol. IV/36: 17 Aug '96 — "Near the end of the tribulation many will die from the comet and its tidal waves... **I will resurrect all of My faithful who will have died during the tribulation.** This is the hope I give to all in this time, whether you survive this time or not. My faithful will receive glorified bodies, and return to a beautiful earth that I will have prepared for you."

Vol. V/6: 6 Oct '96 — "Only My faithful will be brought back to life with glorified bodies. You will have time to adore Me and serve Me every day. You will be giving Me thanks continually that you have been graced to be present in this age. This is a message of hope I am showing you, so that My faithful, who have been purified, will enjoy their reward in My splendour of My Kingdom."

Vol V/7: 7 Oct '96 — "Those who have died and are resurrected, will have glorified bodies and will live to the end of this era. Those, who are faithful and live through the tribulation will have their reward also in My era of peace. **These will have their bodies rejuvenated and will live long lives.** It is only some of these people who may see death before the end of this era. Do not be concerned over the details of how My will intends things."

Vol. XIV/66: 23 Feb '99 — "At the end of My Era of Peace, I will resurrect every body that existed, so that they could be reunited with their souls at My last judgement. Then the eternity of My heavenly court will begin, where all My faithful will witness My beatific vision. You will then share in My love and My peace where only I can satisfy your soul. Rejoice, My people, that you will live to see My day of glory."

God the Creator:

26 Nov '99 — "My people, you have called Me Lord, Jesus, Son of God, or God in praying to Me and asking for My help. When you speak of God, there is no higher force, because I always exist with no beginning. Anything that exists has been created by Me and is formed by My will and exists through My will. I am showing you My power in perspective, even to the devil. I am asking you to give praise to your Lord because I am the one who made you and planned your life.

- The devil tempts you with things that comfort the body but not the soul. *He does not love you, but despises you. So do not listen to his lies.*
- I love you so much that I died for your sins on the cross. I am infinite and unconditional love.
- I have given you free will and I desire that you will love Me and serve Me as My angels do.

"When you consider heavenly ecstasy with the love of your Saviour for ever, how could you choose anything else. Do not be confused or distracted by anything temporary in this life. Seek only things that will enrich your spiritual life by following My Will and My Commandments. So when you think of how awesome your Lord is, think also of Me as a personal God who loves you despite all of your sins and imperfections. **Struggle in your prayers and share in My sacraments so you will have the graces to make it to heaven.**"

God's Plan:

Vol. X/38: 2 Feb '98 — "It is your free will choice to discover who you are and how you fit into My master plan. Everything that happened to Me on earth was planned as well. All of My plans have been revealed to you by prophecy and all of them had to be fulfilled in My time on earth. So it is with the present age. My prophecy in revelation is still being fulfilled as the end days will soon bring an end to this era of evil. Once I have removed the evil ones and all the consequences of Adam's sin, you will see a new earth.…"

Golden gate of Jerusalem:

5 Dec '99 — "My people, a day is coming when I shall return through the golden gate of Jerusalem. I have made this promise in Scripture and that is why many have their burial place opposite this gate. The fact that I am showing you this vision is a sign that My coming again will be soon. Many great things have to happen before you will see Me coming down to the earth again. This means that the tribulation time of the Antichrist is about to begin."

Guardian angels:

Vol. III/45: 21 Aug '95 — "When you are blessed and your soul is not dead to mortal sin, your angel, if requested, will fight the demons for you. This is why it is important to keep pure, by constant confession so you will not be in a weakened state of mortal sin. **Those so disposed to mortal sin will not allow their angels to help them.** Then, the demon of their soul will bring other demons in, and the last state of that man will be worse than the first…"

Healing:

Vol. II/37: 9 Aug '94 — "My people, you are all potential healers. This is a ministry I gave My apostles. If you have strong faith and believe in My power, you will indeed be able to heal people by praying over them in the Holy Spirit. So do not hide your gifts under a bushel basket, but be ready to share your gifts with others.…"

Vol. X/20: 16 Jan '98 — Mary said: "… all those who come to the caves for protection in the tribulation. You will call on the Lord **and He will cause a spring to come forth** to provide you with water to sustain you. Even more miraculously, you will see that this water will provide **healing properties for all who are ill and drink of this water.…** Give thanks to God for all He does for you both now and in the trial to come."

Vol. XII/24: 21 Jul '98— "I am showing the caves deep in the earth where you will find hiding places from the Antichrist. There will be **springs of healing waters** both for drinking and to heal your sickness.… When you see the chariots burning, it is a symbol for you that My angels will keep you from harm. The evil men will not be able to reach you, no matter how sophisticated their devices are. My angels will wrap their arms of protection around you, so the evil demons will not be able to attack you.…"

Heaven: The road to

2 Sep '99 — "My people, as you go down the road of life, you choose the right way or the wrong way to follow. I have told you many times that the road to hell is broad and paved with many good intentions. **The road to heaven is narrow and on that road you will realise your good intentions by your good deeds.** There is a large difference between thinking of doing a good deed and performing the action by your courage and conviction. Follow Me and imitate Me in your actions and you will find yourself at the gates of heaven."

Hell: Many souls go there

Vol. I/212: 3 Jun '94 — "… Many people, when they die, cannot believe it has happened and as a result are not prepared for heaven. **Many souls go to hell because they think they have plenty of time to get spiritual later** and continue on the road to worldliness. It cannot be this way for My faithful. I must be first in your lives at all times, such that you are always prepared if your death…"

6 Sep '99 — "Many souls going to hell are due to these sins of the flesh and unrepentant abortions. The evil of your land is so great, that you are about to face chastisements you have yet to endure. Your freedoms and possessions will soon be stripped from you as you will be brought to your knees for your sins. Because your society has not shunned this sinful behaviour, your children have seen this activity as acceptable behaviour. You are robbing the innocence of My little ones and you will pay for mocking My laws. Be prepared spiritually…"

Herod's edict:

Vol XIII/46: 2 Nov '98 — "An edict will be announced [by Antichrist] as Herod's edict to kill all the babies under two. Only this edict will demand death from all who will not worship the image of the beast. There will be many martyred who will not worship him."

Hibernation: during the tribulation

Vol III/318: 7 Jun '96 — "My children, during the trial, I will help you to induce this phenomena **so you can hibernate for long times without food.** This will help you, since you cannot buy food then, and it will protect you from the evil ones, who are seeking you. Pray to Me for help and I will show you this protection. **Do not be concerned about the details of how I will protect you, but have trust and faith.** You are precious in My eyes and I will see to your needs. My children, pray for discernment and I will always lead you to safety."

Hiding: going into — See also P35 - "The Need to go into hiding"

Vol. III/328: 17 Jun '96 — "My people, **why do you have trouble believing that you must flee into the wilderness?** You want to believe, but still you are attached to your possessions and you fear the unknown. Have no fear, My friends, for this will be a joyous time of faith in My protection. You must be as My apostles when I asked them to follow Me. **You must be willing to drop everything at My word, and follow your angels as I lead you.** I tell you, there will be some trials, but you will see this as a preparation in faith to lead your new lives on a renewed earth.… When you begin to understand My way of perfection, you will ask yourself: 'How could I have been so blind?'"

Vol. VII/41: 15 May '97 — "Look to the signs of [1] the warning, [2] My Pope's exile and [3] this mark of the beast to know when to go into hiding. When you see these events, do not hesitate to go or you may risk being captured and attempts will be made to force you to worship the Antichrist. Fear not, for I will be with you."

Vol. VIII/57: 21 Aug '97 — "My people, on the day I called My apostles to follow Me, I did not ask them to bring all of their possessions, but to walk in faith.… **You are to go into hiding with what you can carry.** Be prepared most for your spiritual attacks with many sacramentals. **Take your rosaries, crucifixes, holy water, Bibles, and blessed candles.** Be prepared to leave your houses and cars behind. The more you trust in Me, I will provide for your physical and spiritual needs. It is this trust in My protection that will guard you. If you do all this for My name's sake to avoid the evil one, your reward will be seen in My Era of Peace."

Holy Communion: Our true daily bread

28 Nov '99 — "My people, each day I feed you with your daily bread to nourish your body. Do not worry that you will find food for yourselves, because I will see to your needs. I have told you how I feed My birds of the air, but you are worth more than a flock of sparrows. Your true daily bread is My Consecrated Host in Holy Communion which nourishes your souls with the grace of My real presence. *For about fifteen minutes you are like human tabernacles with My real presence.*

"For each day you come to Holy Mass and Holy Communion you are feeding your souls and bringing yourselves closer to the day that I will receive you into heaven. **You have the bread of angels because I am in your midst.** Even the angels are jealous of this intimate contact with your Lord. Therefore, after you receive Me in Holy Communion, you should take adequate time to share My love and listen to My words of discernment. It is this special time that you share with Me that will help you to grow in your faith and to learn how to follow My will."

5 Dec '99 — "In Holy Communion you become totally immersed in My Mystical Body by sharing in My real presence. You always have Me present through the power of the Holy Spirit who sustains your existence. **In Holy Communion I manifest Myself to you in a way that makes you feel the closest you can come to heaven on earth.**

- My love and My peace envelop your soul with a grace of My presence that inspires you to want to do everything for Me.
- This peace of Mine is what draws you to want to visit Me at adoration or My tabernacle.

- This love of Mine is that burning desire in your soul that makes you want to be with Me as often as possible.
- This is the love that your soul yearns for to be satisfied.
- Your love for Me is elevated to its highest point when you receive Me in Holy Communion. That is why many of My real faithful lovers desire to receive Me daily at Mass in Holy Communion.

"Those who love Me are not coming out of habit, but crave My real presence more than anything else on earth. Those devoted to Me in such love will receive their heavenly reward every day and for eternity in heaven."

Holy Spirit:

Vol. XII/24: 21 Jul '98 — "I am the Spirit of love.... Call on your heavenly helpers in Me, the angels and the saints. We are all here to answer your requests for protection. For in the trials that you will face, **I will be the One to speak through your lips** and I will give you the grace and the strength to endure this battle. Even if you must suffer and die for Jesus, I will be at your side to sustain you."

Holy water:

Vol. VIII/82: 14 Sep '97 — "My people, when you come into church, you need to bless yourself properly with the holy water. Do not make it a trite gesture. Holy water, properly blessed, has the grace to keep the demons away from you...."

Homosexuality:

Vol. XIII/110: 27 Dec '98 — "**I created you male and female** to be joined as one flesh in marriage.... In the family I have given you a blueprint for the survival of your society. Your marriages or unions of homosexuals are an abomination in My sight."

8 Aug '99 — "**A new threat to family life** is because of your society's acceptance of various sinful lifestyles **as homosexual**

couples and heterosexual couples living together without marriage. When a society does not realise they are living in sin, you are seeing a total breakdown in the moral fibre of your country. Your sin is reaching to Me as the angels witness your abortions and rampant sins of the flesh."

6 Sep '99 — "My people, you have heard My account of creation when I created man and woman to be taken as man and wife and the two would be as one flesh. I later gave you the Ten Commandments **declaring sex outside of marriage to be a serious mortal sin.** Now, today in your country you see **many men and women living together in sin without marriage.** Even some men and women **are living with the same sexes in homosexual sin.** These sins of the flesh are rampant in your society and you are steeped in your pleasures oblivious to how much you are offending Me."

30 Oct '99 — See "Sin". Also "Sin: perverted lifestyles"

Houses of prayer:

Vol. I/46: 9 Nov '93 — "Events will speed up dramatically as the demons take power... **Those houses where prayer is said constantly, I will protect from the flames** — but woe to those houses that do not pray. Fires now in the west will pale in comparison to what will be coming. Some of this can be mitigated by prayer but not all. Start as many prayer groups as possible to stem the tide of the coming evil...."

Human life:

Vol. V/27: 26 Oct '96 — "It is bad enough that you are killing your babies, but still society has yet to accept that they are even human. When you declare it a human at birth, **at which point in your own development do you consider yourself less than human?** You are human from conception, since you came from human parents. Your society denies the unborn is human, so it can justify taking their lives. This killing is a grievous sin, and it becomes a sin against the spirit, even more so, when you refuse to accept it as a sin of murder. If you are to be saved, these sins must be confessed and forgiven."

11 Jul '99 — "Every life **from conception is human and made to My image and likeness.** How would you feel if your mother had decided to abort your life? Many times you do not understand the seriousness of your decisions. I am asking you, My friends, to help educate these women to keep their babies and not to kill them."

24 Nov '99 — "My people, many women who find themselves with an unwanted pregnancy feel like they are trapped in a corner. Some are quick to think of an abortion because of their embarrass-ment or the care and money of raising a child. *Remember that each baby is not really a part of your body and it is human from conception.* There is nothing you can value in place of another life. That is why killing a baby by abortion is equal to killing someone with a gun. You have the responsibility of conceiving the child as much as you have for taking care of this child.

"The doctors also are responsible for protecting life instead of taking money for abortions. This blood money of the doctors is the thirty pieces of silver they take for their acts of killing. I will see to it that this wealth will cause these doctors nothing but grief if they do not repent of their killings. These doctors and lawyers encourage the women to have so called 'safe' abortions, but they will pay for their crimes. Pray for these mothers, the doctors and your representatives that could remove these laws allowing abor-tions. Do everything you can to protect My babies or your country will pay for this blood on your hands. **My cup is overflowing with your sins and My justice will be carried out in your chas-tisements.**"

Information:

11 Aug '99 — "I am showing you in this vision of a spoon that **I only give you a little information at a time** and only what is necessary for you to know at the time. It is what you need for your soul that you are given, but not more than you need or could un-derstand. **So let Me choose what and when to inform you of**

things. Questions to explain what has been given are understood, but questions of things to happen are not your concern. Keep close to Me in prayer...."

Insects: see "Plagues"

Internet: See also P44 - "Electronic communications"

Vol. III/23: 28 Jul '95 — "As your communications and transactions become international, you will see the stage set for the coming of Antichrist. When he comes to power, he will rule the world through your purse strings. As your Internet becomes more inclusive, **you will see how he will send his messages over TV to all households with receivers.** He will mesmerise people with his eyes and his lies. His promise of peace to everyone will draw many to believe in him, but it will be lacking in love. By the time people realise his real intentions of power, it will be too late, since he will control their food and jobs."

Jerusalem:

Golden gate of Jerusalem: 5 Dec '99 — "My people, **a day is coming when I shall return through the golden gate of Jerusalem.** I have made this promise in Scripture and that is why many have their burial place opposite this gate. The fact that I am showing you this vision is a sign that My coming again will be soon. Many great things have to happen before you will see Me coming down to the earth again. **This means that the tribulation time of the Antichrist is about to begin.**"

Temple at the wall: 16 Dec '99 — "My people, **when you see any construction of a temple near this wall in Jerusalem,** you will know the time of the Antichrist is at hand. Many armies will assemble in the Holy Lands hoping to claim these lands for their own. I will come in their midst in triumph with My chastisement and I will claim the earth for My victory. All the evil ones will be banished from My sight into hell."

Jobs:

Vol. XII/19: 16 Jul '98 — "My people, look around at your factory jobs disappearing, as your buildings begin to rot. You are seeing the self-destruction of your industrial might. The one world financiers are pillaging your country of its most important wealth and that is its people. The laws and favoured agreements that your leaders were allowed to make have enabled your employers to trade your jobs for cheaper ones with no concern for their workers. The greed for money and earnings in your stock market will be your ruination. Your greed will fall in on you as your financial empire will collapse under the weight of its own sins."

Judgement: those in mortal sin

Vol. I/87: 3 Jan '94 — "Be always prepared to die on any given day, for I will come as a thief in the night. Those who commit mortal sins should seek confession as soon as possible. **Unless there are unusual circumstances of My Mercy, most souls called home with mortal sin will be sent to hell.** So be on your guard and go to confession often to stay prepared."

24 Jan 2000 — "I am coming to cleanse all evil from the earth and **woe to those who are not prepared for My judgment.** Those who refuse to accept Me as their Saviour and refuse to seek My forgiveness will be the ones to suffer the most on earth and in hell. Heaven rejoices over even one soul that you can bring to conversion. So focus your time on prayers for sinners, teaching My Gospels, and inviting all to My forgiveness of their sins.

"This is an urgent message that I have shared before, but as your time runs out, there will be many souls lost. **Work to save as many souls as you can from Satan's armies.** You can only achieve this through My grace and that of the Holy Spirit. Pray that the harvest master send more labourers into the harvest before My justice comes to the earth."

Kneeling — at the consecration: See "Consecration"

Life — the gift of:

29 Dec '99 — "My people, it is difficult for you to understand why some people are taken home in their younger years. Life is full of unknowns and accidents that cannot always be explained. When you see such a death, this should be a sign to you how fragile and vulnerable your life is. All the more that **you should appreciate the gift of life and that every day should not be taken for granted.** Each day is precious because it gives you a chance to witness your love to Me and to those around you. These events of death should inspire you to make the most of your little time on earth in storing up spiritual treasures and preparing for your own day when you must leave this world."

Lists of Christians:

Vol. XIII/59: 14 Nov '98 — "The evil ones will have **lists from your churches** on who is Christian. The Antichrist will try to force people to take the mark of the beast, but you must refuse his every enticement, even if it means giving up your life."

Low level satellites:

Vol. VII/76: 18 Jun '97 — "My people, be aware that men will be racing to put their low level satellites in orbit very quickly. This competition is to gain control of the communications between the banks and the chips. Once this network is in place, the Antichrist will use it to link the world with him. I am with you always, My children. Pray for My help in these times and I will guide you."

Luminous white crosses:

Vol. VIII/8: 7 Jul '97 — "In the time of the tribulation there will be special places of My holy ground ... For at these places of apparition and holy ground, **the angels will protect you** where the luminous white crosses will be located. In every age I watch over My people in a unique way with My presence."

Vol. XII/70: 1 Sep '98 — "As the time of the tribulation draws near, these evil men will be spreading disease germs in rural areas where they suspect My faithful will be hiding. You will be protected by My angels at all of My safe havens and the caves from any sickness. **Look on the white luminous crosses or drink the healing waters at the caves and you will be healed of any plagues or diseases**. You will be safe at these places from any weapons or detection equipment. Have trust in My help … Pray for My help at all times and your souls will be saved."

Magnetic poles: See "Earth orbit"

Mail monitoring:

Vol.III/27: 2 Aug '95 — "As the evil days grow closer, you will have to **be more watchful of what you send through the mail, and what you say over the telephone**. Evil people will be giving such information to those preparing to persecute you."

Mark of the beast: See also P18

12 Oct '99 — "My people, the message that I have emphasised over and over is to warn the people **not to take the mark of the beast in the body** and not to worship the beast of the Antichrist. I have requested you over and over to give My warning message wherever you go, even if it is an unpopular message. People have asked how the general population will be made aware of this knowledge of the mark of the beast. I have sent My messengers out **to proclaim this warning from the rooftops** without worry of criticism. You have this same word in My Scripture for those who believe and understand this message.

21 Jan 2000 — "My people, those who believe in Me and reject the Antichrist will suffer much persecution in your jobs and buying and selling. Without the mark of the beast in your body, **you will not be able to buy or sell anything. The money used will have the mark of the beast's image on it**. Without this chip in your body, you will not be able to hold jobs, buy food, travel on aeroplanes, or cross borders. Your movements will be restricted for anyone the evil one world people cannot track. Some will be martyred as examples to others whom the evil ones want to control."

Mars Lander:

4 Dec. '99 — "My people, man is being confounded in many of his technological attempts. The difficulties in communicating with the recent Mars Lander is another case in point. It is not with certainty that man knows how everything works. When things fail, it is more a sign of man's fallibility to humble himself. **If everything went smoothly all the time, man's pride would get too puffed up and he would think that he is greater than Me."**

Masons:

Vol. XI/25: 23 Apr '98 — "My people, the Masonic Order is led at the top by very powerful and influential men. They run companies or world organisations that affect the lives of all men and women. These are not only rich people seeking after money, but they also are seeking worldly power. In addition, this group is very much into worshiping Satan and follows the rituals of the occult with special attention to certain numerology. **These are the ones setting up the United Nations to control the world.** Through international financiers they control the money and the heads of state. These will be the ones to cause your religious persecution. They will be the ones also preparing the way for control by the Antichrist.

"They are the one world people setting up **the smart cards and the mark of the beast** in preparation for the new world order. They will be setting up secret lists to do away with all those that stand in their way to rule over men. Pray, My children, for the souls of these people, for their hearts are cold and hideous. Have no fear of them, for My faithful I will protect from the devil's clutches."

11 Jan 2000 — "**The Masons will be responsible for obliterating My consecration** so that it will become an abomination of sacrifice to Satan and the one world religion. When you see this take place, only attend the Mass I have instituted and supported by Pope John Paul II."

Mass: See also P91 - "Masses - Underground Masses"

11 Oct '99 — "My people, the persecution of your priests will be increasing all over the world. You will come to a time when the churches will not be able to hold Mass. **Your priests will have to do secret Masses in your houses.** That is why I have advised you to have all of your Mass items available. When you come to a house at night, you will park your car down the road and walk in the back door. You will use low candle light so you are not so visible. Your prayer groups will have to be run in secret and possibly in places away from the cities.

"As the Antichrist's agents seek out the Christians, **you will eventually have to go into hiding** as I have warned you. Evil will have its hour, but it will only last a short time before I will vanquish all the evil in the world. Once My victory is brought about, you will see My faithful enjoying My Era of Peace on a renewed earth. Rejoice as your persecution heightens, because you will know My coming is at the door."

11 Dec '99 — "My people, you have **a treasure in the Mass beyond comparison**.

- The Holy Sacrifice of the Mass is a gift of My love and My real presence.
- You have the most perfect prayer in the Mass and it is the center of your faith and your community.
- You have My sacrament of Holy Communion to give you the grace to carry you through your day.
- You have the miracle of transubstantiation from the bread and wine into My Body and My Blood.
- You have the Scripture readings and homilies to understand how to live your lives."

22 Jan 2000 — "My people, once the priests omit My proper consecration of the Mass, your churches will be headed downhill. **My**

presence in the Host will no longer be there when the Mass becomes an abomination. From that point on, you will see the one world religion of ecumenism take over. It will reach a point when these evil priests will worship the image of the beast on the same altar that they offered the Mass. Modernism in My Church has already caused some division in the traditions and reverence of My Eucharist. The later stages of the apostasy will become very obvious to everyone. **As soon as the consecration prayers are violated, it will be the beginning of the end.**

"You would better search for a proper underground Mass than partake in what will become a demonic ritual. I have given you the signs of this schism in My Church. **Heed My warnings** and leave these churches of abomination so you can save your soul from this evil influence. Stay faithful to your belief in Me and follow My commandments. Pray much for strength in your time of tribulation because you will be tested in many ways."

Mass kits:

30 Dec '99 — "My people, a time is coming where your churches will be closed to offering Mass. This religious persecution will cause you to have Masses in the homes when a priest is available. This vision of a tabernacle in the home means at that time My faithful will have to protect My Blessed Sacrament from desecration by the evil ones. I will always be with you in My Blessed Sacrament even throughout the tribulation. **I have asked you to prepare Mass kits in your homes for this time.** Even if you cannot have a Mass, you can call on Me in Spiritual Communion and My angels will deliver My host on your tongue.

"**Relics, crucifixes, rosaries**, and holy water will be your sacramentals to protect you from the power of the evil demons. **Have these in your possession at all times.** Some of My faithful will be martyred for your faith, but do not worry since you will be brought straight to heaven. **All who call on My help will have their souls protected in this trial.** So have no fear of the evil ones, for My power will vanquish all of them. You will suffer only a short time since I will do this for the sake of My elect."

Messages:

Vol. III/37: 13 Aug '95 — "Many wish to see what you see and have not seen it, or hear what you hear and have not heard it. It is only when you **see with the eyes of faith and hear with the love in your heart,** that one understands the messages I am sending."

Vol. IV/28: 10 Aug '96 — "Many times I have advised you to seek out caves for protection from the evil men, during the tribulation. **Some have scorned this message from their pride and their fear**. You know how much I love you and that I would not mislead you.

Vol. VII/10: 12 Apr '97 — "While Noah was building the Ark and gathering the animals, there were many people who scoffed at what he was doing. Even now, **you will see many scoffers as well**, criticizing your preparations.

Millenarianism: See also Catechism of the Catholic Church — No. 676

Vol. VI/84: 27 Mar '97 — "The leaders of My Church have made **binding interpretations of 'millenarianism'** which I wish to acknowledge under obedience to My Magisterium. They have not interpreted one thousand years to be taken literally. I will not then reign in My body. Only spiritually will I be present.... Suffice it to say now, when the time comes, you will experience the truth as I have willed it."

Miraculous cures:

Vol. X/97: 27 Mar '98 — **"At the safe havens and caves, all of your sickness will be miraculously cured."**

Miraculous signs:

Vol. VIII/58: 21 Aug '97 — "My people, **be careful to test all the miraculous signs** that will be given to you. Satan will try to imitate My crosses in having them strangely appear. Test the fruits of the spirit at these places. Trust more in crucifixes that have My corpus on them. The evil one cannot witness to My suffering on the cross. **When you hold up My crucifix, it will reveal to you if a miracle is from Me or Satan.**"

Miraculous springs:

Vol. X/20: 16 Jan '98 — Mary said: "My dear children, you have seen many times how signs are given to witness heavenly miracles. Just as the grotto in Lourdes was given for healing waters, you will see this again demonstrated to all those who come to the caves for protection in the tribulation. You will call on the Lord **and He will cause a spring to come forth to provide you with water to sustain you.** Even more miraculously, you will see that this water will provide healing properties for all who are ill and drink of this water. This will be another extension of the mercy of God on all His faithful children… Give thanks to God for all He does for you both now and in the trial to come."

Mobile phones:

"Vol. XIII/18: 13 Oct '98 — "Military people **already carry personnel locators** for when they would be lost behind enemy lines. This same technology could be placed on everyone, so the evil men could follow your every movement. These devices are battery powered and over set time increments emit a microwave signal registering a number associated with each person.

"By using your cellular phone receiving towers, authorities could track every person all over the country and even throughout the world wherever these towers reside. The data is then transmitted to satellites and a network could follow wherever these chips are carried. **Your cellular phones and pagers already tell the authorities where you are**. You would be wise not to use such devices and not to take any of these chips under your skin as the smart chip. By not giving allegiance to the Antichrist, you would be free to travel into hiding places."

Moon — blood red:

Vol. IV/70: 19 Sep '96 — "When you see **the moon turn blood red,** it will be a sign to you of the tribulation among you."

Mortal sin: See "Sin"

New York:

Vol. II/186: 22 Jan '95 — "... *I saw a huge tidal wave come up and envelop New York City. It seemed higher than most of the buildings. The Lord led me to believe this was during the great chastisement.*"

Nuclear weapons:

25 Dec '99 — "My people, you have been singing many Christmas carols about peace on earth, but **how serious is man when it comes to carrying out the peace that I desire for man?** To have My peace would mean that you would have to give up your greed and no longer take things by force in war. Peace is easy to talk and sing about, but it is another thing to be a real peacemaker. There is still a major rift between the Western countries and the communist Eastern countries. **You still have enough nuclear weapons between you to destroy the earth.**

"**It is ironic that your computer problems may make your weapons erratic or even possibly unusable.** There is a true danger though if they should malfunction and could destroy cities by accidental launchings. This is also true of other nuclear weapons in other countries and those possibly in the hands of terrorists. I continue to request your rosaries to stop any war using nuclear weapons or other mass destruction biological weapons. If there is not enough prayer, you could see some serious threats to your survival. Keep focused on My peace of Christmas and pray for peace in your world."

Observation:

21 Jan 2000 — "My people, you are all on a stage of life as you pass your days on earth. Remember that I and all the saints and angels are watching your every action each day. **Even your relatives in heaven are watching you**. So do not disappoint them in bad behaviour, but make them proud of you in all of your good deeds. The woman in the tomb represents St. Agnes and how beautiful all of My faithful will look when one day you will be resurrected in your glorified bodies. Life on earth passes very quickly and soon you will be with Me in paradise. If you love Me, you will do everything to please Me in your daily prayers and actions. Follow My Will in all that you do, and you will have eternal life with Me in heaven."

One world people:

20 Jan 2000 — "My people, **the one world people have controlled your heads of state for many years.** Money runs your world and those in control of your money will control many people's lives. The evil ones will try to use fear and punishment to control everyone in their jobs and their buying and selling. **Do not listen to those trying to force their one world religion on you.** Instead stand up to them and defend your belief in My name, even if you are persecuted in your jobs, your money, or your lives."

Origins of man:

Vol. IX/5: 4 Oct '97 — "My people, I am showing you [as in the vision] about your origins from the first man. Many of your theologians have taken liberties in their interpretation of Genesis. I have told you before that the creation account is the belief that I have revealed to you. **This vision of humanity descending from one man is true and it is not meant to be debated.** Do not be concerned with the gender of terms when you read these accounts. I have made you male and female and every soul is equal before Me."

Permanent sign in the sky:

Vol. I/30: 16 Oct '93 — "There will be a miracle of a permanent sign with the cross in the sky. It will be visible to all and it will be a supernatural event to witness God's presence on earth. Those of faith will praise it and thank God for this precious visitation. Others will refuse to believe in it and will hide their faces from it."

Persecution:

16 Dec '99 — "My people, a time is coming again when the blood of martyrs will be falling on your own land. A religious persecution is already underway against Christians in a subtle way. **A time is upon you when a one world religion, devoid of God, will be forced upon you.** Those who publicly proclaim My name will be sought out for execution. At the same time the mark of the beast will be forced on the people. **Those refusing to take these chips in their hand or forehead will be sent to detention camps.** You have signs of these happenings all around you."

20 Jan 2000 — "My people, just as I was tried unfairly, they will drag you into court and **you will be accused unfairly because of your belief in Me and your denial to worship the Antichrist.** There will be no real justice on this earth until I come again on the clouds of judgment. My justice will soon reign over these evil ones who have claimed their own authority. Rejoice when My day of glory will be seen by My faithful and I will vanquish all of the evil ones."

21 Jan 2000 — "My people, those who believe in Me and reject the Antichrist will suffer much persecution in your jobs and buying and selling. **Without the mark of the beast in your body, you will not be able to buy or sell anything. The money used will have the mark of the beast's image on it.** Without this chip in your body, you will not be able to hold jobs, buy food, travel on aeroplanes, or cross borders. Your movements will be restricted for anyone the evil one world people cannot track. Some will be martyred as examples to others whom the evil ones want to control."

Personnel locators:

Vol. XIII/18: 13 Oct '98 — "Military people **already carry personnel locators** for when they would be lost behind enemy lines. This same technology could be placed on everyone, so the evil men could follow your every movement. These devices are battery powered and over set time increments emit a microwave signal registering a number associated with each person.

"By using your cellular phone receiving towers, authorities could track every person all over the country and even throughout the world wherever these towers reside. **The data is then transmitted to satellites** and a network could follow wherever these chips are carried. **Your cellular phones and pagers already tell the authorities where you are**. You would be wise not to use such devices and not to take any of these chips under your skin as the smart chip. By not giving allegiance to the Antichrist, you would be free to travel into hiding places."

Pets:

13 Jan 2000 — "Jesus said: "My people, many have close relationships with their pet animals for comfort and protection. For those who have wondered about taking them to My refuges **be assured they are part of your family and they are welcome.** As I provide for your food and protection, I will also provide for your pets as well. This is one more reaching out of My love to all of you from wherever you are in life.""

Plagues: See also P42

29 Apr '99 — "My people, your drought and bad weather will continue to worsen until your crops will be endangered. **You will see a chastisement of insects that will attack your fragile crops**. Pray, My children, that you will find enough to eat during a coming world famine. I have asked you to store one year's supply of food and water for when it will be scarce. Pray that enough people will heed My words of warning. I will multiply what you have, if you would just have faith in My word."

Pope John Paul II: See also P10 - "Pope John Paul II and the imposter pope"

Vol. I/213: 4 Jun '94 — **Mary gave a message:** "I have interceded with My Son to protect him [Pope John Paul II] from harm.

Do not be surprised if he is exiled and that it may occur on the thirteenth of some month in the future. There will be political upheaval at that time in Italy which will precipitate his exile."

Vol. V/15: 15 Oct '96 — "This new pope, who will replace Pope John Paul II, will be deceptive and lead the people as a tyrant. He will be trying to use his office to promote the Antichrist. Once you recognise the evil in him, you will remember My words, how he will utter abominations and blasphemies. Be watchful, for **soon you will see his election in violation of the proper succession of popes**. This imposter is not to be obeyed, but reject him, since he will be in league with the Antichrist."

Vol. VI/30: 1 Feb '97 — "My people, I have sent you My Pope son as a special grace, especially for this time. **I ask you to follow him** and listen to all of his decrees and writings. He is the one to teach you faith and morals as given to you from My apostles. This is the line of succession of St. Peter that I have promised to protect My Church."

Vol VI/52: 22 Feb '97 — "There will indeed be a special election controlled by the evil element of the cardinals. **My Pope son will be forced out of office** and the new false witness will bring a schism into My Church. I am telling you My people to follow My traditional teachings and do not listen to the misguiding imposter pope."

Vol. X1/49: 14 May '98 — "There will be a great celebration in the Church before the coming of the Antichrist. **Many will be cheering Pope John Paul II for a while.** "Then evil will prevail over Rome for a short time. It will be My triumph later that will usher in My renewed earth …"

Vol. XIII/23: 17 Oct '98 — "My people, I am preparing you for the time when a schism will occur in My Church. This is a difficult message, but one you need to hear and be aware of. **The next elected pope will occur while My Pope son, John Paul II will still be alive.** My Pope son will be exiled and an evil pope will assume his position. He will change the Mass and many laws with his decrees, but they will violate My tradition and the faith passed on by My apostles. Pray for discernment."

Vol XIII/64: 19 Nov '98 — "My people, I have told you **that an evil man will illegally be elected 'Pope'** and he will control all the churches. He will eventually try to force My faithful to worship the Antichrist, even in My churches. That is why My remnant will leave the churches under his control and go to underground Masses in their homes and other places."

Vol. XIV/5: 5 Jan '99 — "My people, you are comfortable in your churches today, but you are witnessing many changes in My Church all over the world. In your area there are certain quarters trying to deal with an artificial shortage of priests. **Many churches are about to be closed under the guise of 'not enough priests'.** If you encouraged and nurtured vocations, there would be no shortage. These same quarters are changing My interpretation of Scripture for their own hearing. These are the same people who are not in full support of your present Pope John Paul II. **Pray for him, as by his own admission, he will be leaving soon.**"

Vol. XIV/64: 22 Feb '99 — **"My people, I am showing you how My Pope son will be leaving Rome to form an underground church.** Another will take his place after forcing Pope John Paul II into exile. **The black knife [as in the vision] indicates that the Antipope will have evil roots and he will have diabolic designs to change My Church. He will cause a schism in My Church by his evil decrees."**

Preparation:

Vol. V/93: 27 Dec '96 — "**I keep telling you that no one will survive** [the tribulation] without My help. Those who refuse to prepare for this battle with evil will be found wanting and unprepared. It would be better for you to be spiritually prepared, since you will need all of your spiritual weapons, as the rosary, to fight this battle."

Priesthood:

9 Jan 2000 — "My people, you have been asked to pray for vocations to the priesthood this week. Having ministers of My sacraments are very important for the spiritual lifeblood of My Church. I have told you previously how your vocations are down because **you do not encourage or foster vocations in your families.**

"The Holy Spirit moves many to My ministry, but they are not given role models to imitate, nor are priests given the honour they should have in taking My place on earth. Prayer to encourage these vocations to come to fruition is very important and it is needed the year around even beyond praying for one week.

"Beg the harvest master to send workers into the vineyard for souls. The one in the vision symbolises the vocation you may be praying for. **One such generous soul is a prize in any parish and worthy of your prayers.** The lack of priests is yet another symptom of the weakening in the faith of your people. You have a battle going on for souls and the more you ask for My help, I will see you are sincere and answer your prayers."

Resurrection: See "Glorified bodies"

Revelation: Book of

Vol. XII/32: 28 Jul '98 — "My people, I am showing you that this evil age is upon you and the evil one is spewing his hatred upon mankind. **You are living the last book of My Revelation** as the Antichrist is about to assume his brief reign."

Rapture: See "Taken up by God"

Rosaries:

1 Nov '99 — "My people, My mother is holding her rosary to encourage you all to **pray the fifteen decades for her intentions.** First on her list is to be constantly praying for peace in a world that is full of hate and war. Do not let other distractions keep you from praying your rosaries. **Do not put it off to late at night when you may forget to pray them or you may be too tired.** Pray your prayers during the day with a high priority.

"Many evil people in the world are working toward the world's destruction or its takeover. You will have to deal with the age of the coming Antichrist, but **pray in earnest that your nuclear weapons are not used.** If enough prayer is sent to heaven, this scourge of destruction could be mitigated. Listen to My mother's pleas for her rosaries before it is too late."

Russia:

Vol. III/95: 21 Oct '95 — "Beware of the evil roots which lie in Russia. These will be called up once again during the tribulation. The Antichrist will use Russia's armies in his service to try and defeat the good forces in the world, but my angels will come to lead My strong faithful in a final battle with the evil one."

Sacramentals:

Vol. XI/30: 28 Apr '98 — "My people, I am showing you how you need to have your sacramentals on your walls at home. **Have them blessed and place a crucifix, a statue, or an icon in every room of your house.** In that way, no matter what room you are in, you will have remembrance of Me and the saints. Even if you could have a holy water place at your entrance, it would help drive the evil spirits away...."

Safe havens:

Vol. XIV/16: 14 Jan '99 — "My people, I have told you that you would be protected at My places of holy ground and places of My mother's true apparitions. You are seeing [as in the vision] **the angel that will be visible at My safe havens.** Their power will be great over the evil ones and the people will witness My glorious triumph. Rejoice that you are living in these wondrous days."

Satan: See also "Zero population growth"

24 Jan 2000 — "My people, in the innermost recesses of your soul a daily battle is raging in the spiritual life with the evil one. **Do not be over confident in a temporary victory over Satan**, because he is always laying his snares to trap you in your pride and anger. Pray to Me constantly every day for help and rely on Me more than yourselves to fight off evil temptations. If you do happen to fall in serious sin, you can come out of the darkness by confessing your sins in confession. **Do not despair in your sins or give up in laziness,** but struggle to cleanse your sins in My forgiveness and mercy. If you do not struggle toward the light of My salvation, you will be an easy prey to Satan, who is seeking your demise.

"Come to **the One who loves you and reject the lies and promises of the evil one who hates you. It is your choice whether to live in the light or live in the darkness.** Choose carefully because you are considering your eternal destination."

Scanning devices: See **"Cameras"**

Schism:

11 Jan 2000 — "I have promised to protect My Church, but you will still be tested by a schism that will split My Church. No matter how much you will be persecuted for proclaiming this schism, it is your duty to warn My faithful of the Mass being changed in its words so My real presence will no longer be there.

"**The Masons will be responsible for obliterating My consecration** so that it will become an abomination of sacrifice to Satan and the one world religion. When you see this take place, only attend the Mass I have instituted and supported by Pope John Paul II.

"For those praying for My help, I will lead and bless your soul and guard you from these evil people of the coming tribulation. Do not be misled by this one world religion ecumenism which will be a demon in sheep's clothing. My priests have been given authority to consecrate My hosts properly and they will be responsible for carrying on My traditions. **If any priest defies My authority in a**

wrongful consecration, you are not obligated to recognise this as an authentic Mass and Holy Communion.

"These are strong words, but remember that you are dealing with My real presence and I will not be mocked."

Second Coming:

Vol. III/137: 1 Dec '95 — "As the readings [at Mass] indicate, **you will read the signs of My second coming. They are there in scripture for all to read and understand.** When you see an increase in earthquakes, knowledge, apostasy, and omens in the sky, know that My coming is near. First, you must face this evil age in the tribulation, then My glorious victory over evil will bring you to My reign of peace."

Vol. X/34: 30 Jan '98 — "My people, I have given you many messages to watch for the signs in the sky as the end days approach.… I tell you, My people, be on guard because My adversary will try to deceive you with his own signs and wonders, which the Antichrist will be allowed to perform. If someone comes and claims to be Me, do not believe them. **Only when I come on clouds in great glory and the evil ones flee before Me are you to believe that it is My second coming.** "

Sequence of events:

Vol. XIII/94: 13 Dec '98 — "My people, I am showing you this vision because your events are about to take off in rapid fashion. The events leading up to the Antichrist's takeover will be put into motion.

- **That means the warning first**, followed by a short time for meditation and forgiveness.
- **Pope John Paul II will leave Rome**, starting a schism in the Church with the election of the antipope, who will worship the Antichrist.
- **Then people will be promoting the mark of the beast** with a new money system to follow.

- **Chaos will then come with either from a war, a stock crash, or a depression,** whichever the one-world people could easily precipitate.
- **Then the Antichrist will come on the scene**, as the people will choose him as a leader to get them out of their woes.
- Evil will seem to be winning, but only for a short time, **and then My comet of chastisement will strike you as I will triumph over Satan.**"

Sex — outside of marriage:

6 Sep '99 — "My people, you have heard My account of creation when I created man and woman to be taken as man and wife and the two would be as one flesh. **I later gave you the ten commandments declaring sex outside of marriage to be a serious mortal sin.** Now, today in your country you see many men and women living together in sin without marriage. Even some men and women are living with the same sexes in homosexual sin. These sins of the flesh are rampant in your society and you are steeped in your pleasures oblivious to how much you are offending Me."

Shortage of supplies:

12 Aug '99 — "My people, as you will see more divisions occurring in your society, **people will be fighting over the short supplies** of necessities. A police state will come over your country and the military will take control of all the food, fuel and airports. There will be large fences as people will try to protect themselves from their neighbours. These riots and fights over the necessities will be one of your signs to consider going into hiding at that time."

Signs:

20 Jan 2000 — "My people, **many have refused to believe that they are in the days right before the great tribulation of the Antichrist.** I have witnessed to you the signs in your weather, your earthquakes, and the control of your computer chips in your buying and selling. I told you how when you see the trees budding and the weather warming, you know that spring is about to come. So, also, when you see the apostasy of your world, rampant sins against My commandments and signs in the skies, you will see the evil age of the Antichrist about to take over the world. Fear not, My people, for I will protect you against evil influences and I will provide for your needs. **Do not use these evil chips to buy and sell,** but put your full trust in My protection."

Simultaneous events:

Vol. II/18: 20 Jul '94 — "I have told you before how events will occur so fast it will seem many of them are simultaneous. What is happening is a convergence of things coming together in concert right up to these end times."

Sin:

Vol. I/86: 3 Jan '94— "You should try to stay in the state of grace always for you do not know when I will call you to judgement. Be always prepared to die on any given day, for I will come as a thief in the night. Those who commit mortal sins should seek confession as soon as possible. Unless there are unusual circumstances of My mercy, **most souls called home with mortal sin will be sent to hell.** So be on your guard and go to confession often to stay prepared."

Vol. II/P65: 7 Sep '94 — "You must remember that **all sins of the flesh are serious mortal sins** and require confession to be forgiven. They are abortion, contraception, pre-marital sex, fornication and adultery. Avoid these sins under pain of loss of My grace. People are still committing sin, even though they do not think so. Without being sorry for your sin and admitting how it offends Me, you cannot be My disciple. Your will must come into conformity with mine if you choose to want me in heaven."

Vol. VIII/90: 21 Sep '97 — **"Sinners do not want to be told of their sins,** since they will no longer be able to have their bodily pleasures. For those that want sin to be revealed to them, let me show you things some do not even think are sins:

"Having **intercourse before marriage; using contraception** even when you are married; **masturbation** and any other **unnatural means to prevent conception such as vasectomies and tying of the tube in women.** Other sins concern **ruining other's reputations with gossip, slandering others, cheating employees out of their just wages and benefits.** Whenever you violate My Ten Commandments as in doing harm to your neighbour or not worshipping Me on Sundays, your need to be sorrowful for your sins and seek My forgiveness of them."

Examples of *Mortal Sins:* **9 Oct. 1999** — "My people, **any taking of life is the most serious sin you could commit against Me.** Life is the gift I give each soul at conception and this plan I have for every life should not be violated. That is why all sins connected with life are mortal sins.

"Abortion, homicide, euthanasia, suicide, and even sexual sins are mortal sins. When you use artificial insemination, birth control, or any other artificial means of transmitting life, these also are mortal sins. All sins of the flesh in masturbation, sex before marriage or outside of marriage are mortal sins. These sins require being confessed in the sacrament of reconciliation to be forgiven."

30 Oct '99 — "My people, this is the cup of My wrath and it is spilling over and calling on My justice. I am merciful and loving, but I am also just. Your country has reached a point of decadence and sin that some do not even admit they are sinning. **If you need an example of your sins, let Me list them for you:**

- Many couples in your country and other countries are living together without the bond of marriage and see nothing wrong.
- You are seeing lesbian and homosexual couples seeking rights for marriage and adoption.
- There are unfaithful spouses committing fornication with each other and prostitutes.
- There are many rapes and abuses going on even within the family's own members.
- Abortions, euthanasia, and planned killings are occurring every day.
- Drug abuse, drinking and other addictions are being encouraged by the availability of these substances."

Sin: Perverted lifestyles: 1 Dec '99 —

"My people, **I want to speak to you of two lifestyles that have perverted My union of spouses and are occasions of mortal sin:**

- A man and woman living together without marriage are just as much sinners as those living together in a homosexual union. I created them male and female to be joined in marriage with Me in the center of that marriage bond. **A couple living together for pleasure and no responsibilities are committing a mortal sin in every one of their unions.**
- **Sex without marriage violates the sixth commandment** and you will have to make reparation for each of these sins. Again, **homosexual unions** are also outside of a proper marriage and **are an abomination in My sight.** If such people violate My laws and do not seek forgiveness, they will be condemned to hell. My mercy awaits each sinner to their dying day, if they would only repent. I condemn the sins you perform and not the person. But to continue in such lifestyles, it is an occasion of sin you should remove yourselves from.
- **I condone proper sexual union only under the marriage bond of those two partners joined in union with My sacramental grace.** For people to perpetuate living together or having homosexual unions, you do not only cause sin in yourselves, but you give bad example to others who see this as an acceptance of sin as justified. My justice will continue to see these unions outside of marriage as sinful and in need of repentance.

So come and **follow My commandments** by living properly under the marriage bond. Pray for those in these sinful lives and encourage them to have a proper marriage. Reach out and love these misled people and admonish them for their sinful behaviour. You have a responsibility to reach out and save sinners, even if they refuse to listen to you."

Souls of relatives:

Vol. XII/28: 23 Jul '98 — "Your blessed sacramentals will protect you from evil spirits in your trial. Have faith and hope in Me that my mother's mantle and My arms will wrap our protection around your souls. Have faith in praying for your relatives' souls as they will be spared My justice for your sake."

Spies — in prayer groups:

Vol. XII/50: 13 Aug '98 — " My people, the evil ones will try to send spies among your prayer groups and meetings. The cross on your foreheads will only be present on My faithful. So, check all of the foreheads of your number to find the spies who do not have this cross. This is another gift I will give you to avoid being captured."

Smart card:

4 Aug '99 — "My people, I am showing you how evil this age is going to be as the Antichrist will try to force everyone to worship him. This will be closely linked with the chip that they will try to force you to take in the right hand or the forehead. **To reject the worship of the beast and refuse to take his mark is requested very clearly in the Book of Revelation.**

"I have asked people in My messages **to even refuse taking smart cards.** It is better not to be influenced by the advantages of the smart card to enter your job, use cellular phones or certain satellite antennas. If you do not have the smart card, you would not be tempted when they try and force you to next take a chip in your body for security.

"You would be better to quit jobs or schools who demand smart cards and get other work or go to other schools."

13 Jan 2000 — "You will see continuing preparations to encourage the people to take smart cards and even chips in the hand. All this will be done to make way for the Antichrist and his control of buying and selling through the mark of the beast. Do not be fearful of these events because I will protect My faithful. **Refuse to take the mark of the beast for jobs or food, but rely solely on My angels' help.** Again, when you cannot receive Me in a Mass, call on Me in Spiritual Communion and during the tribulation I will send My angels to place a Host on your tongue. I will be present with you, but remember to call on My help since you will not resist the Antichrist on your own."

13 Jan 2000 — "My people, **the Internet and your satellites are dominating your communications and your purchases more and more.** Be aware, My children, of the control of your jobs and your transactions by smart cards and other devices that use satellite positioning for their directions. **This gradual control over your daily lives should be another sign to you that the Antichrist is near** to exploit these world wide connections. As more rely on these chips for daily survival, this is why I have asked you not to take the smart cards so that you are not under the control of the evil one."

Stars — conjunction of: See "Conjunction of stars"

Taken up by God:

Vol. III/84: 8 Oct '95 — "… I will take **some of My faithful up** with Me before the three days of darkness. The remaining faithful will be fighting in the Battle of Armageddon or safe in the caves. This moment will be the downfall of Satan's legions as My angels will then chain them in hell. It will be the culmination of the earth's purification. **All of My faithful will then be drawn up as the earth is renewed.**"

Vol. III/276: 30 Apr '96 — "… Right before I renew the earth, I will take My faithful up to a safe place… As you are carried off, I will renew the earth to a paradise you cannot imagine…"

Telephone monitoring:

Vol.III/27: 2 Aug '95 — "As the evil days grow closer, you will have to be more watchful of what you send through the mail, **and what you say over the telephone.** Evil people will be giving such information to those preparing to persecute you."

Television: See also "Warning"

Vol. IX/61: 29 Nov '97 — "My people, I wish to warn you about the coming of the Antichrist and his declaration. At the time of his first announcement about his coming in declaration, **have all of your cables out of your house and do not watch your television any longer — disconnect them.** As it comes closer to the day of his declaration, do away with your **telephone lines, your computers, faxes, copiers, radios, and anything electronic** that can be influenced by the demons, since they will use them to distract you. In addition, stop your newspaper and even your mail. All of these will be controlled."

Vol. XV/40: 4 May '99 — "My people, you have reached a new level of terrorism when you have to be concerned about your children carrying weapons. How many lives are going to be lost in your schools until your society wakes up to what your children are being exposed to? The violence on TV and in your movies has been a plague beyond pornography. **Your computer age has given too much information to those who want to destroy and kill.** You have become a violent people with homicides at a high level and many abortions every day. Wars are ongoing in many countries at any one time. Is it any wonder that such a violent culture will breed children killing each other?

"**Turn off your televisions and boycott your violent movies** and you will take away the money from those perpetrating violence. Stop your wars and killing babies and you will take the blood-money away from the arms makers and the doctors. You need to **pray much to protect your families** from being infected with your anger-driven death culture."

14 Jan 2000 — "These beams will send TV signals of the Antichrist to all the televisions in the area and **you will see his face on the screen even if your set is not turned on.** Those with chips and TVs will be influenced to worship the Antichrist and use his money and his food. I told you after the warning to **get rid of all of your TVs and computer monitors** so you could not see this evil man's face."

Temple at the Wall: See "Jerusalem"

Test all miraculous signs:

Vol. VIII/58: 21 Aug '97 — "My people, be careful to test all the miraculous signs that will be given to you. Satan will try to imitate My crosses in having them strangely appear. Test the fruits of the spirit at these places. Trust more in crucifixes that have My corpus on them. The evil one cannot witness to My suffering on the cross. **When you hold up My crucifix, it will reveal to you if a miracle is from Me or Satan.**"

Tribulation: See also P49

Vol. I/27: 9 Oct '93 — "You will suffer through demonic forces **for three and a half years.** The faithful will be forced underground like the catacombs. Some will be martyred, but fear not, for I will strengthen and protect My little ones. In the end My Sacred Heart will triumph."

Vol. IV/70: 19 Sep '96 — "When you see **the moon turn blood red,** it will be a sign to you of the tribulation among you."

Vol. XII/45: 9 Aug '98 — "When the tribulation approaches, **as signaled by the warning,** take your TVs out of your houses and do not be influenced by watching the Antichrist."

Vol. XV/42: 6 May '99 — "A time of tribulation will come about, but My power will quickly vanquish Satan and his demons. The evil of your world has gone beyond the point of no return, as in the time of Noah. Prepare your spiritual lives and be ready to receive Me, as I will come in triumph."

20 Nov '99 — "My people, I have told you that My faithful will have to suffer much during the tribulation in your persecution. **The tribulation will be a purification as a suffering of purgatory on earth in the body.** At the same time, the evil and unfaithful souls will have to face the wrath of My judgment. I am merciful, but just and I give you much opportunity to change your ways after your life review of My warning.

"Those who still refuse My love and mock My laws will have to pay the price for their disobedience. Those who take the mark of the beast and give praise to the Antichrist **will have to suffer a living hell in the body before they are chained in hell forever.** You are seeing one of the many plagues that these evil souls must suffer. They will roam for days in an inferno of flames that will not consume their bodies. **I will rain fire down from heaven and they will not escape the torture of these flames.** I have told you that the wages of sin are death, but there will be an eternal suffering of pain as well."

13 Jan 2000 — "My people, **the vision of this candle** snuffed out and completely melted to the base **indicates the time of your tribulation is not far off.** It means your time of apostasy is well on its way and soon your churches will be an abomination to Me **as they will be used for one world religion services. As you** saw the Israelites defeated even with the Ark of the Covenant in their midst, so My faithful are about to be tested in like manner even with My Host in your midst. Because many do not even believe in My real presence, what you have had in My Eucharist will be taken away from your churches."

20 Jan 2000 — "My people, **many have refused to believe** that they are in the days right before the great tribulation of the Antichrist. I have witnessed to you the signs in your weather, your earthquakes, and the control of your computer chips in your buying and selling. I told you how when you see the trees budding and the weather warming, you know that spring is about to come. So, also, when you see the apostasy of your world, rampant sins against My commandments and signs in the skies, you will see the evil age of the Antichrist about to take over the world. Fear not, My people, for I will protect you against evil influences and I will provide for your needs. **Do not use these evil chips to buy and sell, but put your full trust in My protection.**"

21 Jan 2000 — "Call on My help when your tribulation begins and I will have My angels lead you to My refuges. **By a miracle of**

My grace, I will provide your food, shelter, and protection from the evil ones. You may even be threatened with your life to believe in Me, but fear not for I will ease your pain and guard your soul from the evil ones. Trust in Me and follow My ways, and you will have everything provided for you."

The True Church:

Vol. III/105: 1 Nov '95 — "Many religions think they are equal to Roman Catholics, but indeed many are badly mistaken and are being misled. I come to those who seek Me in truth, not by someone's interpreted vision of Me through other religions."

Understanding the messages:

Vol. III/37: 13 Aug '95 — "Many wish to see what you see and have not seen it, or hear what you hear but have not heard it. **It is only when you see with the eyes of faith and hear with the love in your heart**, that one understands the message I am sending. Do not have doubts, My son, when I have shown you the way."

UN troops:

20 Jan 2000 — "My people, your police and servicemen will be challenged in their authority as the one world people implement their plans for takeover. **You will see foreign UN troops gain a foothold all over your country** and they will claim to be in control. This challenge in authority will cause fighting, killing, and chaos in your streets. You may have to leave your cities for your refuges to avoid these evil people claiming to be in power. Pray much in this coming tribulation so you will be strong in your faith."

USA:

20 Jan 2000 — "My people, **many kingdoms before you have fallen** because of their immorality and their sins of the flesh. These nations were strong in battle, but they have fallen from within as they became blind with drink and greed for power. **Your country**

is no different. Your nation was founded on God-given principles, but you will fall to your knees because I will withdraw My blessings. You will fall with the weight of your sins pulling you down. **I have seen your good works, but your abortions and lifestyles will condemn you.**"

Vatican II:

Vol. XIII/47: 3 Nov '98 — "My people, I am showing you how many changes have been brought in because of the spirit of Vatican II, **but really they were disguised lies from Satan.** These errors and the loss of reverence were brought in to you as a good, but they were like a Trojan horse reflecting your times. **It is important to see how your local priests have been duped by Satan and those urging changes.** The priests have become weak in feeding My souls. They should be encouraging confession rather than worrying about their time spent in the confessional. If only a few come, it is because there are no sermons on sin to cause the parishioners to seek the Sacrament of Reconciliation."

Vocation in life:

7 Dec '99 — "My people, when you look to your vocation in life, you are looking at the means to your eternal salvation. **Whether you are married, a priest, or in single life, I am present sacramentally in the midst of your life.** The bouquet of flowers represents your commitment to loving your spouse in marriage or loving Me as your spouse in the religious life. The flowing water represents the graces that flow from my sacramental presence. In marriage remember that I am a third partner in creating new life in your children. My Church is the same image as married spouses because new life in the Spirit comes forth in My followers who believe in Me.

To the married spouses:

- I ask you to treasure the love you have for each other and build it up every day by saying I love you often.

- By actions and words you need to express your love for each other. Do not demean your partners by picking on their weaknesses, even in jest, but build on the good things they do in truthful acknowledgment.
- Look beyond your defects as I do and love the person just for who they are.

"This love of spouses I want you to **take one step further in loving Me**. You know I love you infinitely. But I keep asking you three times, like St. Peter, if you truly love Me. No matter how many times you are tested, I want you to have faith in Me and give Me your yes in all I ask of you. **Whatever you do for My sake, I will multiply your reward beyond what you could ever imagine.** Let Me hold you in My arms as I walk you through life in whatever vocation that you have chosen. I love you and heaven rejoices over even one repentant sinner."

Warning: See also P1 - "The warning"

Vol. XIII/3: 1 Oct '98 — "… as the time of My warning comes, you will see some major signs in the sky that will announce My coming to judge each soul with their life review. Some will be shocked by this experience. That will make each person take notice of their sins…"

8 Oct '99 — "My people, **you will see a major celestial event** when a part of a comet will effect the earth, but not the final chastisement. Many will be frightened by this event, but **it will coincide with My warning experience**. As you all see your sins and how I would judge you, some may be frightened also to see their judgment in how you offended Me."

Vol. III/58: 6 Sep '95 — "At My Warning you will see **an unusual darkness come over the earth as at My crucifixion.** It will be a time to awaken souls not listening to My word."

Vol. XIV: 24 Mar '99 — "My people, I have asked you to look to the skies for the signs of the end times. The warning is coming soon and there will be some celestial signs of its coming. This heavenly sign will be the same sign that I have told you about at the time of the warning. There will be a darkness associated with this event."

Vol. XV/81: 9 Jun '99 — "My people, **I have given you advice not to watch your TVs, especially after the warning**, because the Antichrist will use this as a means to control the people… I am warning you not to look on the image of the beast, not to take his mark, and not to worship him."

2 Jul '99 — "My people, this is a sign to you of the warning experience. You are not on top of it, but it is not far off. I told you before that it will come at a time when you least suspect it. **There will be a buzzing sound because your life review will be passing by very fast.** You will be able to see clearly all of the events in your life. Your preparation for this time should include frequent confession and a daily prayer life.

"At the end of your life review y**ou will see the place in heaven, purgatory, or hell** that has been prepared for you if you were to die at that time. You can change the outcome of this decision when you come back into your body on earth. **There will be time by My mercy to convert your lives**. This may well be the last chance for many souls to be saved from hell.

"It is the prayers and counselling of My faithful that could bring souls to Me at that time. Once the tribulation begins, it will be difficult to change the hearts of lost souls."

19 Nov '99 — "My people, I am showing you this empty baby basket to indicate a new year is coming and another commemoration of My birth is also coming. **This year has had many disastrous earthquakes, fires and storms**.

"**The year to come is even more foreboding** considering your computer problems and more disasters to come. *This coming year* **will reveal more of the plans of the one world people to take over** using the rollover of the next year as an excuse.

"There will be **increasing turmoil and chaos** *throughout the year* leaving your world prone for the Antichrist to take power.

Many of your people will be in a panic not knowing what to do or where to go. **Pray when things turn serious that My warning will be enough to turn many souls over to Me in conversion.** Without My help many souls would fall into the hands of the evil ones. Pray, My children, that you will be spiritually prepared for this coming battle in your tribulation by going to frequent confession and praying your rosaries."

23 Dec '99 — "As a result of [My] love, **I am giving you a second chance in My warning experience to the whole world.**

- Everyone will see a sign in the sky as you will be stopped wherever you are to see a life review and how I would judge your life;
- You will then resume your life but with a word of knowledge about what is truly good and evil;
- You will be warned not to take a computer chip in your body for fear of losing your soul;
- After this second chance to return your love to Me, you will be more responsible for your decision.

"It is during this short time of repentance that My faithful will be helping the lukewarm back to the faith. You will all be given this spiritual preparation so you will be able to endure the coming tribulation of the Antichrist. Give Me your love and commitment and I will protect you from the evil ones in miraculous ways."

Water:

10 Sep '99 — "My people, beware of the quality of your drinking water. **Whether it be from a bacteria outbreak or terrorist poisoning, your water is more critical than you have suspected.** I have asked you to store water because it may be difficult to obtain if your pumps do not work or if your water becomes contaminated. This is just one of the main items you will need in your physical preparations."

Weather:

22 Jan 2000 — "My people, there are many things you take for granted and one of them is heating your home, especially in the northern climates of winter. It costs money for your fuel or other means that you use to heat your homes. There are even charity organisations to help the poor so they do not freeze. The cold works many hardships on people both in travel and getting through the winter. **I have told you that there would be a rugged winter in this season and you are seeing such effects now.** While you are warm in your houses, think and pray for those who are suffering a lot more than you and who may not be able to afford to heat their homes."

Women:

13 Sep '99 — "My people, I am showing you this woman in the workplace to make a point of how your society values its women. Many of your people do not always realise **the value of the woman who stays at home to take care of her preschool children.** You value a person's success by how much money or how many possessions they have. I value a soul by the love in their heart for others and not just physical actions. Some women want to be fulfilled in a working career, while other women desire to fulfill a career as a mother to their small children. **I give more credit to those women who give up financial gain to share their personal loving care with their children**. You cannot replace a mother's love with a babysitter or a health care provider.

"So think twice how you will bring up your children. **Do not let your children be starved for your love and attention.** Many times it is how a child's early formation was carried out that determines how their lives and attitudes are formed. I love you so much as My children and I want you to show your love for your own children as well. **Money does not buy love or attention. It is your own gift of self and your time that will make you good parents.** Pray that all of your families will be wrapped in My love and your own love for each other."

Women priests:

Vol. III/71: 23 Sep '95 — "If I should only call men to be My priests, it is not to say women are not capable, but it is what I have chosen. It is not right that those of different persuasions would want to change My scriptures or treat the Trinity in a disrespectful manner. My scripture and My laws are changeless."

Year 2K problems:

3 Aug '99: "You have been hearing every power plant, most banks and even governments saying they are year 2000 compliant to set the people's minds at rest. The real problem is that they are not telling you the truth and they really are not sure if their fixes will work. They do not want to cause panic now, but they are only postponing the problem until later. Many nuclear plants and coal plants are not compliant and it only takes a few to go offline to cause a breakdown on your grids. Without power many of your conveniences will not work. That is why I have been telling you to **prepare for the worst with food, water, and fuel in colder areas**.

"You will see **a domino effect on even your basic necessities** as power outages could cause disasters and looting. With storms and broiling heat problems your power has been variable. Add your computer problems and imbedded chips to these outages and **you could have serious consequences**."

Year 2000:

16 Nov '99 — "My people, those who are used to watching television programs are going to have some major disruptions. I have told you that you will be stripped of your possessions. **In the coming year you will see many losses in electricity, and transportation and water problems.** I have told you that many of your leaders are lying to you about the computer problems. You will see terrorist activities and planned manipulation of these problems by the one world people. They will use this coming year's change as an excuse for giving them more control over your lives. **You will see shortages in food, water, and fuel**. There is no question that those who do not heed My words of preparation *will be hungry, thirsty, and cold in the northern areas.*"

19 Nov '99 — "My people, the year to come is even more foreboding considering your computer problems and more disasters to come. *This coming year* **will reveal more of the plans of the one world people to take over** using the rollover of the next year as an excuse. There will be **increasing turmoil and chaos** *throughout the year* leaving your world prone for the Antichrist to take power. Many of your people will be in a panic not knowing what to do or where to go. **Pray when things turn serious that My warning will be enough to turn many souls over to Me in conversion.** Without My help many souls would fall into the hands of the evil ones. Pray, My children, that you will be spiritually prepared for this coming battle in your tribulation by going to frequent confession and praying your rosaries."

10 Dec '99 — "My people, many nations around the world have their troops ready if they have to declare martial law. You will see an increasing number of reports about possible failures with your computers. As the new year progresses, many of these failures will come about and it will change your whole way of living.

"Those who have prepared extra water, food, and fuel will be fortunate that they prepared themselves for the worst. Many shortages will cause disruptions in people's necessities before they can adjust to the new way of life. These **disruptions will offer the one world people the opportunity they have been seeking for a world chaos.**"

11 Jan 2000 — "My people, because you have not seen any dramatic problems immediately, you think that I have misled you. **This year will be a turning point in preparation for the Antichrist to come**. Many have accentuated the potential for problems in your computers.

"**Your coming year will have its trials,** but it will come from a mixture of planned conflicts, sun spot related storms, natural disasters, **and most important from a manipulation of control by the one world people.**

"You should keep your focus on the control of your jobs, the use of smart cards and smart chips in the body, and the status of activities in My Church in Rome. **The food and water you were asked to prepare was not just for the beginning of 2000, but for a world famine where food will be short,** and when you do not have the mark of the beast to buy and sell."

Zero population growth:

Vol. XV/34: 28 Apr '99 — "My people, **you need to know that Satan is behind all of the efforts for 'zero population growth,' because he wants to destroy man.** He tries to influence women to kill their babies in the name of women's 'rights' and convenience. Satan has lulled many to believe that babies are only fetuses, or anything but human.

"**In euthanasia**, people are convinced to kill to stop pain or seek only a quality of life. The truth of killing in abortion and euthanasia is never admitted by those making money on this carnage. Satan is also encouraging nations and ethnic groups to fight for land. Again, money is made in weapons, as more lives are taken in these wars. Some evil men are also working on biological warfare, which can kill many innocent people through designed viruses. **Even Satan-worship, evil movies, and evil computer games are influencing your children to kill each other.**

"Once you realise that you are in a battle between Good and Evil, you can see how all of the evil forces are seeking to destroy man. Come to Me, My faithful, with prayer and fasting to fight this spiritual battle which has created your death culture."

Part VI

Preparation to go into Hiding

Why should we have to go into hiding?. 228

What does it mean to "go into hiding"?. 228

How will we know who we can trust in these times? . 229

What will it be like — going into hiding? 229

What will we do in hiding? 230

Where do we go? 231

How do we go into hiding? 233

Can we go together? 233

When do we go? 234

What if we have disabled relatives?. 235

What about families with young children? 236

What should families take with them?. 236

What do we do for food, water, clothes and
    other essentials? 237

What about the day of departure? 238

Preparation to go into Hiding[1]
(Some Suggestions Based on Jesus' Words to John Leary)

Exodus 16:1-4

The whole congregation of the Israelites set out from E'lim; and Israel came to the wilderness of Sin, which is between E'lim and Sinai, on the fifteenth day of the second month after they had departed from the land of Egypt. The whole congregation of the Israelites complained against Moses and Aaron in the wilderness. The Israelites said to them, "if only we had died by the hand of the Lord in the land of Egypt, when we sat by the fleshpots and ate our fill of bread; for you have brought us out into this wilderness to kill this whole assembly with hunger." Then the Lord said to Moses, "I am going to rain bread from heaven for you, and each day the people shall go out and gather enough for that day. In this way I will test them, whether they will follow My instruction or not."

Jesus to John Leary — Vol. II, P100 — 17 Oct '94

"My people, many will be in need of shelter with little time to provide for one. I have told you not to worry about what you are to eat or where you are to stay; I will provide for you. You will see miracles I will perform for you. I will make caves for you if you cannot make one or find one. The same with food. I will provide manna when none is available. I will be guiding

---

[1] All comments made that are not direct quotes of Our Divine Lord's words are advisory only, and are made as suggestions to people who may be concerned about the matters discussed in Part IV.

*your way much like God the Father helped the Israel-
ites in the Exodus. Be confident in Me ... pray for My
help and you will receive it."*

Why Should We Have to go into Hiding?

No one "has to" go into hiding. The choice is yours. If you do
stay in your home, you will have to take the mark of the beast in
the hand or forehead in order to pay for your electricity, food and
other essentials you would need. Without the mark of the beast,
you would starve. You can, of course, stay right in your home and
not take the mark of the beast — until, that is, the Antichrist's
agents come for you and put you in a detention centre, either to
force you into slavery or torture, or to put you to death. The choice
really is yours.

If you have not taken the chip in the hand or the forehead, you
will be an enemy of the Antichrist and your days will be numbered
— unless you go into hiding. If you do take the chip in the hand or
forehead, you will be an enemy of God, you will be forced to worship the Antichrist and you will be in a hypnotic state with no control over what you do. The Antichrist or his agents will be able to
do with you what they want to. In this situation, if you have "knowingly" taken the chip in the hand or forehead, you cannot be en-
tered in the Book of Life and, after a short time, you may find
yourself in the fires of hell for all eternity. The choice is yours.

What Does it Mean to "Go Into Hiding"?

To go into hiding means that you:

1)   have surrendered your will to God so that you subject your-
       self to the Will of God in all things and are obedient to Him
       in all things;
2)   are prepared to allow yourself to be totally dependent on
       God for all your needs — physical and spiritual. There will
       be no point in planning your escape from the Antichrist if
       you do not include Jesus in your plans and, in fact, you do
       not let Him do the planning;

3) must be prepared to leave all your possessions behind (your new car, your wealthy bank account, your beautiful (?) house, whatever else of this life you value) and put all your trust in God;

4) will only be able to take a few essentials (a minimum of clothes, blankets and bedding, a shovel etc) — what you can carry, including, and most importantly, your spiritual weapons — **rosary, Bible, holy water, crucifixes, blessed candles, spiritual books and pictures etc.**

5) must be prepared to go whenever (at short notice — even in the middle of the night) and wherever the Lord's angels lead you.

As Jesus told John Leary (Vol III, P328):

> *"You must be as My apostles when I asked them to follow Me. You must be willing to drop everything at My word, and follow your angels as I lead you..."*

6) must have trustingly prayed to the Lord and your guardian angels to lead you to safety at the appropriate time and have been totally prepared to surrender all to their leadership.

How Will We Know Who We Can Trust in These Times?

Jesus' words to John Leary (Vol. I, P63) tell us that:

> *"You will be branded for Me with a cross on your forehead for all those that are faithful. In this sign you will see those who are true to My word and can be trusted."*

Elsewhere, Jesus has revealed that this sign will not be visible to those who are with the Antichrist.

What Will it be Like — Going into Hiding?

It is important to understand that things may not be easy when you go into hiding.

Jesus' message to John Leary on (Vol. XIV, P49), may give some indication of this:

> *"My faithful, I have told you, will be protected at holy ground places and caves. Those who are unfaithful will have to suffer a living hell on Earth before they are chained in hell.... My faithful will suffer persecution, but not to the extent that the evil ones will be facing. **There will be no escape from suffering**, since this will be your time of purification at the tribulation. Those that follow Satan will suffer immensely, forever."*

Suffering will be an essential part of your time in hiding because, after the tribulation and the chastisement, Jesus will bring about the Era of Peace. Because this can be likened to a heaven on earth for all who have survived the tribulation, prior suffering will have been necessary for any sins for which temporal punishment is due. As there will be no purgatory for those people, the suffering necessary must be undergone during the tribulation. This will, however, also be a time of great joy, for those in hiding will understand that they are in preparation for the wonders of the Era of Peace.

Jesus has also said (Vol. V, P15):

> *"You will suffer much at this time [in the time of the trial], but you need to purify yourselves almost as an earthly purgatory. All your comforts will be taken away and you will have to endure some mundane hardships. **If you did not suffer as I did, how could you be worthy of the gift of life in the era of peace? What else could you offer Me in return for this joy?** This trial will have a redeeming grace for you, so do not complain of any problems you must face."*

What Will We Do in Hiding?

First and foremost, our concern will be to do the will of God. We will, however, have our Bibles and spiritual books as well as our spiritual exercises. So we can draw our own conclusions. Our children will still need to learn and, especially, need to learn about God and develop their prayer life, and we will need to continue our own spiritual development. It will be a preparation time for the Era of Peace. To help with the passage of time, Jesus will teach us how to hibernate for some of the time (see next page).

Jesus told John Leary (Vol. III, P318) that:

> *"... during the trial, I will help you to induce this phenomenon [hibernation] so you can hibernate for long times without food. This will help you, since you cannot buy food then, and it will protect you from the evil ones, who are seeking you. Pray to Me for help and I will show you this protection. Do not be concerned with the details of how I will protect you, but have trust and faith. You are precious in My eyes and I will see to your needs. Pray, My children, for discernment and I will always lead you to safety."*

Where Do We Go?

This will not be of immediate concern. The first and foremost demand on you is to surrender yourself to the will of God. Jesus will have your guardian angels go before you to guide you on your way.

Jesus has revealed to John Leary (Vol. XI, P77):

> *"There will be a physical light as in the time of the Exodus to show you the way to a safe haven or cave."*

You may have to go to a number of places before you reach your final destination.

Jesus has also told John Leary (Vol. VII, P57) that:

> *"Some of these places [refuges] that are known may serve as interim staging areas for the places your an-*

gels will lead you to. These interim places have means to house the faithful and are in the wilderness areas away from the cities. They preserve My Eucharistic Presence. Be grateful for those given to make these sites. Even some sites will be made into final refuges when the angels come to protect the people from the evil ones. Do not worry about finding your refuge, since the angels will find them for you. Pray, My people, for your spiritual strength to live through this purification. Have confidence in My word and My love, since I will provide for your protection."

Jesus has told John Leary (Vol. III, p104) that:

"When you go into hiding, My people, pray to your guardian angel to direct you. They will lead you to safe places in such a way that no evil men will find you. Even if they should try to find you with their electronic devices, I will confuse their instruments. If they should send out tracking dogs for you, I will misdirect their attention and their sense of smell. I will go to great lengths to protect those who pray for My help..."

While some people will find themselves in caves, others may even be in old mines or in the safe refuges and safe havens. Note also **Jesus' words to John Leary on 16 June 1998 (Vol. XI, P89)***:*

"Of the things I have asked you to take, there was a small shovel for such digging [as in the vision]. If the hills you are sent to are all rock, I will have My angels carve out a cave for you. If there is enough ground for digging, you could make your own home where no one could find you. You will be surprised how industrious you can become, to save your life and possibly those of your family as well. I will protect My faithful in many ways and I will feed you in your need."

How Do We Go into Hiding?

If you do not have an older vehicle you may have to walk or ride a bike or get a lift with someone you can trust.

As Jesus has revealed to John Leary (Vol. VII, P39):

> *"... More and more sophisticated devices are being placed in your car for detection devices ... Satellites will be tracking your car's whereabouts..." and* **(Vol. VIII, P39)** *"...many of your newer cars have transponders in them so the evil people may be able to track where you are."*

Jesus has also told John Leary (Vol. XII, P28) that:

> *"... older vehicles will be safer in bringing you to My safe havens. Newer vehicles will only be useful for part of your travel to your refuge destination."*

So newer vehicles are out. You would be wise to purchase a cheap, older car, particularly one that does not have any computerisation as your car with computer chips can be immobilised by the low earth orbit satellite.

Can We Go Together?

Jesus has told John Leary (Vol. II, P123) that:

> *"I am telling you not to fear what will happen for I will be leading you.* ***Do not fear either for others, for I will direct them as well.*** *You may have to split into smaller groups to avoid detection. Where you go you will not be able to take your cars very far, since they are traceable to your whereabouts. Take some basic necessities, but do not worry. I will provide for what you need. The main concern is your care to remain faithful to Me to save your soul. In the end this is all that matters. To survive this time or not is not important."*

We should not be concerned for family members who may be separated from us. Jesus will protect them also and lead them to safety, if we pray trustingly for them. Children under the age of reason will be protected by Jesus from the trials of the Chastisement.

When Do We Go into Hiding?

Jesus has given John Leary three signs of when to go into hiding (Vol. IX, P61):

"Remember, when you see [1] My warning, [2] Pope John Paul leaving Rome, and [3] the placement of the chips in the hand, you are to pack your sacramentals and your physical needs, ready to go into hiding. Do not have any credit cards, smart cards, nor anyone with a chip in their body, since you can be tracked by these devices."

Again, Jesus has told John Leary (Vol. XIV, P64) that:

"When you see My Pope son leave Rome, I have encouraged you to call on Me and I will have your guardian angels lead you to a safe refuge in hiding.[2]

In addition, **Jesus has said (John Leary Vol. III, P292):**

"... I will even give you an urge for your own safety, to go into the hills to hide. You will see how I will provide a shelter for you, away from the evil spirits and the Antichrist's agents. I will blind their eyes to your whereabouts ..."

---

[2] It must be understood that not all people will be taken into hiding. Those whom the Divine Will has marked for martyrdom will find themselves headed in a different direction. It is, of course, a great privilege to be selected by Jesus for martyrdom. Martyrdom should not be feared as Jesus has promised (John Leary Vol. XII, P28) that He will soften the pain of His martyrs and give them the grace to endure it.

Jesus has told John Leary (Vol. III, P241) that:

> *"... many will remain near their homes until they receive some physical evidence when to go into hiding. I have already warned you to go into hiding when the mark of the beast will be proclaimed. You will see signs in the skies... I will provide your food and shelter, if you provide your prayers and trust in Me."*

What if I Have Old or Disabled Relatives?

Jesus has not mentioned the aged or those with disabilities. However, when the time comes to go into hiding, you will, if you have been praying to Jesus and your guardian angels to lead you to safety, find yourself being led by your guardian angel (the physical light mentioned above — see page 181) to wherever you are to go. You will not, therefore, also be trying to reach any relatives you might wish to see taken to safety, unless you are being led by your angel to them. We can only trust that Jesus will be directing them as well (see above: Can we go Together? — page 182).

If you are an aged person or a person who has difficulty in moving about, you need to put your trust in Jesus and pray for His guidance and help and the help of his angels. It would appear, however, that, of itself, age is not a reason to refuse to go into hiding. Indeed, anyone who freely chooses not to go into hiding, runs the risk of falling into the clutches of the Antichrist and surrendering to his charisma and, apparent, miraculous powers.

Therefore, it would seem wise that, in an act of complete trust and abandonment to Jesus' will, you resolve to go into hiding, regardless of your limiting circumstances, and prayerfully trust that the means to do so will be available to you at the time. Were you to stay behind, you would not have any electricity, food, water or other conveniences, unless you take the Mark of the Beast in the hand or the forehead in order to buy and sell. This would then place you in the situation discussed above (see: Why should we go into Hiding? — page 177).

What About Families with Young Children?

Families with young children need to start planning early. They are in a more complex situation than individuals. It would seem, however, that in the family situation, you will not be able to cater for all their needs, you must, therefore, trust in Jesus for His miraculous help, as He has promised (see below). To the extent that you can, you should aim for a minimum of essentials for each family member. Because it will be impossible to get ready to go at short notice, if you have not packed in advance, you should make a list for each person and prepare all that you will be able to carry. You could make small packs for each child to carry, and a larger one each for the parents.

What Should Families Take With Them?

You should not be concerned with trying to take a large number of changes of clothes for the children, nor should individuals for that matter. Jesus has said He will provide for us and we must take Him at His word and place our full trust in Him. It is suggested, therefore, that you do not try to provide for a whole range of summer clothes, if it is winter (or vice versa) when you go into hiding. Cater only for the present but include at least one item of warm clothing and a change of summer clothing. Carry as much underwear as you wish (but be sensible about it) as it is light and can fold up very small. It would be useful to have one change of shoes of some kind, preferably for evening wear to relieve the feet of the pressure of ordinary shoes. If there is not enough room to carry all these things, then don't worry about them. Our Divine Lord will provide where we are unable to help ourselves.

We must realise, that if we try to provide all the comforts of home, our efforts are undoubtedly doomed to failure. The reason is that Our Divine Lord insists that we trust in Him to provide. In fact, He asks us to be like His disciples, when He sent them out with nothing but what they stood up in. If this seems like a contradiction to the above, it is my view that Our Divine Lord also expects us to use our intelligence and provide for ourselves in a limited way.

You might, however, have a sleeping bag for each person and a single small pillow. You may even be able to include a blanket, towel each, face washers, soap, and some other toiletries — and your small shovel! You will also need things like scissors — for hair cutting — a small mirror, hair brush and comb and tooth brush and toothpaste. Radios must be left behind. Their transmission can be tracked.

Remember, do not try to cater long term, it is simply impossible to carry all that would be required — Jesus will provide for our needs, but we must trust in Him and show we do by the things we do not take. It would be wise for each person to have a raincoat — one that can fold up into a small parcel for ease of carrying, and a fold-away umbrella — also for ease of carrying.

It would probably also be wise to include some light ground sheets and, possibly, a rug with rubberised underlay for waterproofing.

As you may have to do some walking before you reach your final destination, you may wish to purchase a luggage trolley, like people have for their suitcases when travelling on planes, and some straps to hold your luggage on.

What Do We Do For Food, Water, Clothes and Other Essentials?

It is essential that we trust in Jesus — He will provide all. But we must stay true to His commands and give Him love and adoration.

Jesus has told John Leary (Vol. III, P289):

> "...You will suffer for a short time, but I will provide water and spiritual food for you to survive. Be willing to follow Me in faith and, with My help, I will bring you into the next era of peace by My victory. Your joy then will have no bounds."

And again, Jesus has said: (Vol. XII, P24 and P58):

> "...I will provide food and water for you miraculously, just as I did for My people in the desert in the Exodus..." and:

> *"...Whatever food you take with you, I will continue to multiply for you. Have total faith in My help..."*

Jesus has told John Leary (Vol. II, P38) that:

> *"...My people, do not be anxious about what you are to wear or what you will eat. For if I care for the lilies of the field and the birds of the air, do you not think I will care for you even during the tribulation?"*

These are very reassuring words from Our Divine Lord. We must trust in Him. Jesus has also said that if we need medicines do not worry, He will provide these also.

What About the Day of Departure?

This is something over which we may have no control. We must be ready at all times to go once the warning has occurred and the Pope has left Rome. We should have our bags packed and ready. Initially, we need to have some drinking water in a bottle for each person (with a strap on the bottle to help carry it), and some pre-packed eats for the short term — depending on what else we wish to carry. After that, we trust in the Lord for our needs and pray for the help He has promised.